NOCTURNE: THE ART OF JAMES McNEILL WHISTLER

ARRANGEMENT IN GREY: SELF PORTRAIT. Canvas (29½ x 21 in.). Signed, lower left, with a butterfly. The frame, decorated by Whistler, is also signed. Painted between 1871 and 1873, when it was exhibited at the Society of French Artists, London (The Detroit Institute of Art).

NOCTURNE:
THE ART OF JAMES
McNEILL WHISTLER

DENYS SUTTON

J. B. LIPPINCOTT COMPANY
Philadelphia • New York
1964

TO CYNTHIA

for her 'exquisite comprehension'

Contents

Illustrations

ILLUSTRATIONS IN THE TEXT

Prefatory Note

OVER a decade ago I started work on a *catalogue raisonné* of Whistler's oil paintings in collaboration with the late J. W. Revillon. For a variety of reasons, among them the death of my collaborator, this task was abandoned. It is now in the hands of Mr Andrew McLaren Young of the History of Art Department at Glasgow University.

The aim of this study is not to discuss the authenticity of Whistler's *oeuvre*, a complicated affair, but to give some coherence to the development of his art and to place it and his ideas against the contemporary background. I have made no attempt to write his life.

Much has been written about Whistler. The student is referred to Don C. Seitz's *Writings by and about James Abbott McNeill Whistler. A Bibliography* (1910), which covers most of the material published prior to that date, and to the valuable annotated bibliography contained in the catalogue of the Whistler exhibition arranged by Mr Young for the Arts Council in 1960 and subsequently shown at the Knoedler Galleries in New York. Reference should also be made to the catalogue of the exhibition *Prélude à Whistler* held at the Centre Culturel Americain, Paris, in 1961.

Any lover of Whistler automatically owes much to the writings of Joseph and Elizabeth Pennell, even though, in some particulars, argument has arisen as to the accuracy of their statements; at times they were certainly touchingly naïve. Nevertheless, their two volume biography and their Whistler *Journal* are lively and highly informative. I have used them constantly.

Whistler's etchings are illustrated in E. G. Kennedy's *The Etched Work of Whistler*, 1910, in four volumes. The same author's book on the lithographs also contains illustrations. For catalogue details concerning the etchings and lithographs, reference is necessary to the publications by Mansfield (for the etchings), issued in 1909, and T. R. Way (for the lithographs), issued in 1905. I have not burdened the present volume by cross-references to these works; in general, I have endeavoured to keep the footnotes to a bare minimum.

I have read a large part of the unpublished material relating to Whistler, principally the letters which he wrote and which are mainly conserved at Glasgow and Washington. I must express my thanks to the authorities of Glasgow University (the holders of the Copyright) for permission to quote from the artist's letters and to those officials at the Library of Congress and the Freer Gallery, Washington, who lightened my task by their kindness.

Thanks are due to the Knoedler Galleries for their loan of colour blocks and to all those private and public collections which have allowed the works in their possession to be reproduced.

My thanks are also due to the late J. W. Revillon, whose draft *catalogue raisonné* has laid the foundation for any study of Whistler's painting; to Mr McLaren Young, who made available to me the material in his charge at Glasgow and who read the book in manuscript; to Miss Mary Anne Norbury; to Mr Peter Tunnard; and Mr John Russell. Mr Theodore Crombie has kindly read the proofs. I also owe much to my wife for her observant criticism.

Chelsea, 1963.   D.S.

Introduction

JUST over half a century ago, many good judges in Europe and America considered Whistler to be one of the major artists of the age. His influence was certainly widespread; and in 1905 he was posthumously honoured by two comprehensive retrospective exhibitions held in Paris and London, while no less a sculptor than Rodin was commissioned to undertake a statue in his honour. Yet within a quarter of a century, his reputation had suffered a severe eclipse. It was his fate to be remembered as a brilliant, if hard-hitting, wit, and as a characteristic figure of the 1890s; but his art, though still retaining some staunch admirers, was barely studied.

For this situation Whistler had largely himself to blame, and for the following reason. He was one of the first artists to have realised that personal publicity can prove extremely helpful in bolstering up a reputation or in furthering an artistic programme. He was keen to do both. His flair for self-advertisement was so developed that, by attracting considerable attention to his own personality, he tended to promote his quirks at the expense of his work. In the end it was Whistler the man, not Whistler the artist, who stole the thunder. Consequently, the story of his life rather than the study of his art has engaged writers. In his own era, the many letters he sent to the press, which took up so much of his time and on which he lavished such care, his brilliant and celebrated lecture, the 'Ten o'Clock', given before a select group of fashionable and intellectual society, his parties and his law suits—all these made him a famous, even a notorious, figure. In an age of poseurs he was one of the most successful, in an age of diners-out, he was one of the most spirited—and one so sure of his prowess as a conversationalist that, when it suited him, he did not hesitate to be most infernally impudent, even turning up for dinner as much as an hour late!

One has to reckon, of course, with the habits of contemporary society, in which a premium was placed on the expression of individuality. Gustave Geffroy, that perceptive and experienced critic, was probably correct in maintaining[1] that Whistler ought to be considered as a typical celebrity of the day and someone as much in the public eye as the Prince of Wales, Gladstone, Henry Irving or the professional beauties, and as a representative of that intellectual dandyism which 'feels quite at home in our topsy-turvy civilisation'. Moreover, as the same writer claimed, he had much in common with a dandy like Barbey d'Aurevilly and, in his

---

[1] In an article of 4th November, 1891, in *La Vie Artistique*, Vols. I–VIII, 1892–1903. Vol. I, pp. 73–85.

opinion, they 'shared the same haughty belief in the privileged status conferred by art, the same bold sensations, the same audacity in their judgements'.

Obviously, Whistler's dandyism deserves to be reckoned with in any study of the man and the artist: it explains much about his attitude to life and about his work and its character. The care he bestowed on his personal appearance was one sign of his self-absorption; the eye-glass, the quiff of white hair, arranged as attentively as one would a cravat, the emphasis upon taste and style, and the costumes he went in for—these were all weapons in the dandy's armoury; not that Beau Brummell would have necessarily approved of his turn-out. In a period when to be well dressed was to be dressed discreetly, Whistler's get-up, almost verging on fancy dress, was as outré as Wilde's; and both men were stamped with the touch of the outsider. But Whistler's dandyism was by no means exclusively sartorial; indeed, his attitudinising was not designed to impress high Society, but to underline the differences existing between himself and other men. Rather in the same way as Baudelaire, he seems to have believed in the emergence and relevance of a new sort of aristocracy, based on the possession of heavenly gifts; and the proud, very revealing and, in some ways, rather sad dedication of his book *The Gentle Art of Making Enemies* to 'the rare Few, who, early in Life, have rid Themselves of the friendship of the Many', demonstrates both his self-sufficiency and his fundamental belief in the existence of, and necessity for, an élite.

It is a sentence which tells us much about the man. The familiar stories about him, those anecdotes which have grown a little rusty with repetition, indicate Whistler's firm attachment to the idea that the world was antagonistic to him and his art and that, at all costs, he had to keep his end up, even at the price of endless and at times ridiculous feuds. This attitude is implied in his remark to his relentless biographers, Joseph and Elizabeth Pennell, that: 'Well, you know, when I first came to England I found I had put my foot in it, and—well—I have kept it there ever since!'[1] We can still hear, I think, the triumph in his voice as he justified his stand.

By no means all his victims were worth powder and shot; some of his verbal attacks, which he found so cutting and brilliant, now strike us as being rather vulgar; but he could not resist letting himself go. This desire to show off may have been partly due to the theatrical side of his character which, on occasion, could come to his aid; for instance, it permitted him to score off Ruskin's barrister at the time of the celebrated trial. On such occasions he knew when to pause and when to offer a gesture; and his devilry is well caught in Max Beerbohm's caricature of him in the witness box at the Sickert-Pennell action in 1897[2] (Fig. 37) which is now in the City Art Gallery, Birmingham. This, the histrionic component in his nature, is brought out in his various self-portraits; and it is hardly surprising

[1] E. R. and J. Pennell, *The Whistler Journal*, 1921, p. 156.
[2] This was drawn much later, in 1926.

to find that in two of the last—that of 1898 in the Birnie Philip Bequest, Glasgow, and that (Fig. 58) in the National Gallery, Washington—he has the air of a rather seedy actor-manager.

Nevertheless, one may sympathise with the sardonic, aggressive strain in his temperament; he was up against an artistic establishment which strongly believed in all he detested. Understandably he saw himself as a knight in shining armour, campaigning for pure artistic ideals, but, in spite of his championship of the 'art for art's sake' principle, he was no willowy aesthete; on the contrary, he was a tough fighter. Yet the opposition he met with aggravated the battling side of his character, and his was a curiously torn, split nature. This is one of the factors which helps to explain the continuing fascination which he exerts—as a human being. He never altogether fitted into the contemporary world; it is the impression he makes of being almost something of an exile in his own time (and owing to the demands of his character) which helps to bring him so close to us today. He was one of those restless artists who never grow roots; indeed, where did he belong? He was an American by birth but he never returned home. He was a resident in England for many years and exceedingly proud to become the President of the Royal Society of British Artists and to receive the Prince of Wales in this capacity; but, inevitably, he took the other side in the Boer War. Typically and proudly, he declared in the few pages of his autobiography:[1] 'To begin with I am not an Englishman.'

His prickly nature was such as to prevent him from successfully captivating London after the manner of his illustrious compatriot, Henry James, who became such a literary and social lion in the 1880s. Whistler certainly made his mark as a 'character' and a feared one at that, but his personality prevented his acceptance on the scale enjoyed by his compatriot. The comparisons between the two men—the one the controversial Bohemian, the other the observant and distinguished novelist—may be a little unfair; yet there can be no charge that Whistler's difficulties arose from anti-Americanism on the part of the English.

He did not fare much better across the Channel. He was a life-long Francophile, but, although his Parisian friends included Mallarmé and Paul Helleu, he was never altogether at his ease in Paris; in short, he was an eternal expatriate. It was in keeping with his character that he once said to the Pennells: 'I do not care for definitely settling down anywhere. Where there is no more space for improvement, or dreaming about improvement, where mystery is in perfect shape, it is *finis*—the end—death. There is no hope, nor outlook left.'[2]

G. K. Chesterton contended that he 'was one of those people who lived up to their emotional income, who are always taut and tingling with vanity. Hence he had no strength to spare; hence he had no kindness, no geniality, for geniality is

---

[1] The manuscript of this short document is in the Birnie Philip Bequest, Glasgow University.

[2] E. R. and J. Pennell, *The Life of James McNeill Whistler*, 2 vols., 1908. Vol. II, p. 94. In subsequent references, this book is cited as Pennell.

almost definable as strength to spare.'[1] There is much in this judgement on him; for, on many occasions, Whistler gave the impression that he was living on a razor's edge and looking for trouble. But he was capable of love and affection. The tone of his letters to his mother is warm and kind; for instance, in a charming note from Venice he wrote: 'Goodbye my darling Mother. . . . I am at work first thing at dawn and the last thing at night, and loving you all the while.'[2] His passionate attachment to his wife, Trixie, is confirmed by his correspondence with her, and he could prove considerate to his friends; this is borne out by Mazzini's words about him to Madame Venturi.[3]

There is a great temptation to poke fun at Whistler, after the manner of Degas, who knew how to cut him down to size;[4] and, in any reappraisal of his contribution, one might feel like dismissing him as little more than a hopeless and adolescent exhibitionist, a megalomaniac and a brash Yankee. By certain real standards, he may be judged rather a rotter, and his rounding on Mortimer Menpes and Sickert, both of whom served him well, leaves a nasty taste in the mouth. Yet, always, we have to remember his artistic integrity and take account of the curious dichotomy which obtained between the outward man and his creative achievement. However much he pirouetted and disported himself in the world, erecting thereby a carapace which hid perhaps the real man, he was a diligent worker; that he would turn up in the morning, spruce and eager to take up where he had left off the day before, is admitted even by his critical colleagues. Also, there is little doubt that he cared more deeply about people and things than he was usually prepared to admit: 'but the reason of the evasion,' declared Max Beerbohm,[5] no sparer of human foibles, 'was reverence. He kept himself reverently at a distance. He knew what he could not do, nor was he ever confident even of the things that he could do; and these things, therefore, he did superlatively well, having to grope for the means in the recesses of his soul.'

There was a streak of paranoia in his make-up. He may have suffered from the realisation that, as an American, he was cut off from the old world to which he so much wished to belong, and this may have given him an added determination to make his mark in it; and, at the same time, he realised how much he could contribute to art. Above all Whistler was an aesthete and, as a consequence, he eventually tried to render his art as rarefied as possible and to introduce an aesthetic note into his surroundings out of protest against the materialism of his epoch.

---

[1] 'On the Wit of Whistler' in *Heretics*, 1905, p. 238.

[2] Cited by Elizabeth Mumford, *Whistler's Mother*, 1940, p. 247.

[3] See a letter of 31st August, 1868, in *Mazzini's Letters to an English Family*, ed. E. F. Richards, 3 vols., 1922. Vol. III, p. 200.

[4] As Sir William Rothenstein said: 'Degas was the only man of whom Whistler was a little afraid'. For some anecdotes concerning their encounters, see *Men and Memories*, 2 vols., 1931–32. Vol. I, pp. 101–2.

[5] 'Whistler's Writing' in *Yet Again*, 1909, p. 112.

Yet although seeking novel means of expression he was not unmindful of tradition. And he took immense pains; this is substantiated by his mastery of the technique of etching and by the nature of his pictorial experiments. Now that his personality has afforded the theme for so many books and essays, it is high time that his art was re-examined. For, in the long run, it is his art, not his character, which is important and lasting.

❦ ONE ❦

Between Two Capitals

WHISTLER, who was born at Lowell, Massachusetts, on July 14th, 1834, of Scottish ancestry, was already a cosmopolitan in his youth. He lived as a boy in St Petersburg, where his father, a distinguished civil engineer, was engaged on railway construction for the Russian government and subsequently, in 1848, he spent a short time at school in England. Originally he was destined for the army, and to this end attended the crack United States Military Academy at West Point—a fact of which he was almost inordinately proud in later years. He made a number of drawings and caricatures at this institution; but was discharged for his deficiency in chemistry. For a time in 1855 he stayed in Baltimore, where his mother had taken a house, and while there he experimented with lithography.[1]

He then served for a short spell with the United States Coast Geodetic Survey, where his principal task was to etch maps and topographical plans. His real bent, however, lay in the direction of painting and in this year he threw up his post and took a studio in Washington where he painted a few portraits.

At this period the American scene had little to offer Whistler, and his artistic career, properly speaking, began only when he arrived in Paris in November, 1855, on an allowance of 350 dollars a year. He was one of the growing number of Americans who looked for their training to the Paris studios. Understandably, Parisian life itself held numerous attractions for him and, like many a young man, before and since, he plunged happily into the excitements of the Quartier Latin

[1] A unique lithograph, *The Standard Bearer*, with the inscription on the reverse *J. Whistler, fecit. Baltimore*, 1855. *17th July to Frank B. Harper* is in the Library of Congress, Washington; see *Quarterly Journal of Current Acquisitions*, xi (1953), pp. 30–3. This is close in style to another lithograph which carries the caption in his own handwriting 'Engaged man sings. . . . Dearest wilt thou then as now.' See A. Hyatt Mayor, 'An Early Whistler Lithograph' in *Print Collector's Quarterly*, xxiv (1937), pp. 305–7. *The Standard Bearer* also carries some resemblance to the drawings which appear in a letter written in 1855 from Baltimore to a friend in Stonington. The artist possibly executed these lithographs in one of the numerous lithographic establishments in Baltimore, which included Sachse and Company and Hoen and Company; it might have been designed as the cover to a popular song, as at this date the city was the centre of music publishing in the United States.

for which his temperament, no less than a reading of Murger's *Scènes de la vie de Bohême*, which came his way before leaving home, thoroughly disposed him. He had one advantage over many of his fellow countrymen in so far as his French was relatively fluent—the legacy of his early stay in Russia where he had learnt the language. The anecdotes relating to his student days in Paris are as well known as they are expected. *The Self Portrait* (Fig. 1) in the Freer Gallery, Washington, shows him wearing a sort of *chapeau artiste* and reveals his bohemianism. In true romantic fashion, he lived with a young milliner named Eloise, known as *La Tigresse*, who served as the model for the charming etching *Fumette* (Fig. 7); and in a no less romantic fashion, she tore up his drawings in a fit of rage.

Many of Whistler's friends at this time were English and, for a short spell, he shared rooms with L. M. Lamont, a fellow student at Charles Gleyre's academy and the model for the character of 'the Laird' in George du Maurier's celebrated novel *Trilby*. Besides Lamont and Du Maurier, his circle included Thomas Armstrong, whose memoirs[1] provide some valuable impressions of him in the Paris days; E. J. Poynter, who studied under Gleyre; Joseph Rowley, who appears in *Trilby* as 'Taffy'; and Alecco Ionides, 'the Greek' in the same book. The story of 'the Laird', 'the Greek', 'Taffy' and 'Trilby' herself still has an appeal, and in its sentimental way captures something both of the customs and the mood of the young foreign art student living in mid-nineteenth-century Paris. Not that Whistler altogether fitted into this group; already he seems to have been rather a law unto himself; and it was probably typical of the impression he made on his companions that Du Maurier later saw fit to introduce him into his novel as Joe Sibley, 'the idle apprentice'.[2]

This interpretation of Whistler is a characteristic example of the way in which many of his contemporaries misread his nature. Naturally, much depends on what is meant by work. For one thing, Whistler was not a conventional student; he was not prepared to accept all he was told; he was by no means shy about giving rein to his artistic impulses; and he was quite ready to look in unexpected directions. In fact, his student days in Paris underline the sharpness of his powers of observation and his awareness of fresh experiences; and these, in Paris, could be found on every side. Also, he was the sort of quick-witted person who, in a rather effortless fashion, picks up a great deal, certainly more than is often suspected at the time by his more pedestrian friends; such was his flair. In the main, of course, he did much as the others; for instance, he executed the well-nigh regulation copies after Old Masters in the Louvre for which he had received a commission from an American client, and his choice included Boucher's *Diana at the Pool*, Ingres' *Angelica*,

---

[1] *A Memoir, 1832–1911*, 1912.

[2] Joe Sibley only appears in that portion of the novel, Part 3, which was serialised in *Harper's Magazine*, lxxxviii (1894), pp. 567–87. After Whistler protested, Harper's apologised and 'Bald Anthony' replaced Joe Sibley in the text published in book form.

1 SELF PORTRAIT.

Canvas, 18¼ × 15 in. About 1857–58. Signed 'Whistler'. Freer Gallery of Art, Washington.

2 AT THE PIANO.

Canvas, 26 × 35½ in. Begun 1858; rejected at the Salon of 1859. Cincinnati Art Museum, Ohio.

3 HARMONY IN GREEN AND ROSE: THE MUSIC ROOM.

Canvas, 37⅝ × 27⅞ in. 1860. Freer Gallery of Art, Washington.

Veronese's *Marriage Feast at Cana*, and Velasquez's *Cavaliers*.[1] He drew, rather
in the manner of Gavarni, scenes from local life and put in some attendance at
Gleyre's studio. This broadening-out process was doubtless assisted by his meeting
various French students at Gleyre's, among them Henri Martin and Henri
Oulevey, a painter; at this stage, he also came across Becquet, a musician, Drouet,
a sculptor, and Ernest Delaunoy, an artist. Such contacts were highly important
for him; and not only artistically; they also meant that he became familiar with
modern French literature and thought; later on the writings of Baudelaire, for
instance, profoundly influenced his own aesthetic ideas.

Whistler had arrived in Paris at a singularly exciting and vital moment. Briefly
put, the main artistic trend of the day consisted of a reaction against romanticism
and classicism in favour of realism; consequently much painting—in particular that
of Bonvin, Courbet and Manet—was characterised by low tonalities, a keen
interest in *facture* as such and an absorption in everyday subject-matter. No doubt
the feeling that one could paint in a bold, broad manner was infectious enough;
but not the least of Whistler's achievements was his swift understanding of the
artistic temper of the hour. He was in the movement. And like many of his contemporaries, he grasped the relevance of seventeenth-century Spanish painting,
particularly the significance of Velasquez.

His love for Spanish art brought him right into the centre of the new artistic
revolution, with its emphasis on the painterly values. *Hispagnolisme*, the taste for
Spain and her civilisation, had already been apparent in the work of French
eighteenth-century painters like Fragonard and de Troy, and this taste[2] had
received wider diffusion at the hands of the romantic generation: Gautier, Hugo
and Merimée were all devotees of Spain so that by the end of the 1830s *Hispagnolisme* had become a popular craze. Although in the 1840s this fashion was
partly on the way out, the marriage of Louis-Napoleon to a Spanish beauty gave it
a new lease of life; and, at the same time, Spanish painting excited the radical
artists. Whistler was thus well placed to share in this revival of taste for Spanish
art, which was equally widespread in England, where various publications on
Velasquez by Richard Ford and Sir John Stirling-Maxwell appeared in the
mid-century. It was in accord with this new found enthusiasm that in the summer of
1857 he travelled with Henri Martin to Manchester in order to see the famous
Old Masters exhibition held there, which included fourteen paintings by, or
attributed to, Velasquez, among them the celebrated 'Rokeby' Venus, now in the
National Gallery, London, as well as various works given to Goya and Zurbaran.
Yet although later on he had every intention of visiting Madrid, he never actually

[1] A fine chalk drawing of a Cavalier after Velasquez ('Souvenir of Velasquez'), formerly in the possession
of H. Graves, is reproduced in Pennell, I, opp. p. 104.

[2] For a good short account of the nineteenth-century taste for Spanish art in France, see J. Richardson,
Edouard Manet, 1958.

got there; however, for a receptive artist this did not matter so much; once he had discovered Velasquez, he could find what he was looking for simply by examining such pictures as were available in London and Paris or at the Manchester exhibition.

The Spanish painter's example counted greatly with many men between 1850 and 1870; Manet, Carolus-Duran and Sargent were among those who admired and studied this master, not to speak of R. A. M. Stevenson, that painter turned art critic who published a brilliant volume on him in 1895. Velasquez provided the painter with a precedent for the use of low tonalities and for neutral coloured backgrounds, employed in order to set off the principal figure or figures in a composition; above all, his pictures indicated how each portion of the composition could be related to the other by means of tonal painting and consequently seen from a single angle of vision as an impression. These were Whistler's own aims and understandably he never wavered in his affection for the master; indeed his studio effects included a number of photographs after his works. Yet although always a faithful follower of Velasquez, Whistler avoided the pitfalls of pastiche; his great predecessor's example stimulated him and urged him to emulation.

Whistler's stay in Paris was also important in so far as it introduced him to some of the main artistic principles current in the 1850s. In later years, his own practice as a painter suggested that he derived considerable nourishment from the precepts of Charles Gleyre and the theories of Lecoq de Boisbaudran; the last, which were only published in 1862, would have reached him through his friends Fantin-Latour and Alphonse Legros, both of whom had been pupils of this teacher. Gleyre, a glacial academic painter, was to have through his hands some of the most brilliant artists of the day, among them Renoir and Monet who, needless to say, liked neither his teaching nor his work. Whistler, for his part, was equally un-enthusiastic about his painting; nevertheless, his subsequent attitude may well have been shaped by the sort of observation Gleyre is said to have made to Monet: 'Nature, my friend, is all right as an element of study, but it offers no interest. Style, you see, is everything.'[1] From this teacher, too, he may have derived his habit of arranging the colours on the palette in the order in which he wished to use them when starting work on a picture; and just as Gleyre maintained that 'ivory black was the basis for tonal painting' so Whistler himself affirmed that black was 'the universal harmoniser'.[2]

Lecoq de Boisbaudran had argued[3] that a painter should not be concerned with the literal appearance of the model; he should be trained to draw from memory in order to facilitate his quest for originality; this would develop in him a feeling for life and the art of representing forms in poses not found in the studio. Such a

[1] Cited by John Rewald, *The History of Impressionism*, 1946, p. 60.   [2] Pennell, I, p. 50.
[3] The *Education de la mémoire pittoresque* appeared in 1862. A convenient edition of this theorist's writings was published in 1920.

method, he claimed, not only stimulated the imagination but served to unleash it. 'The relations', he declared, 'between the memory and the imagination are so direct and immediate, that it is generally acknowledged that the imagination does no more than fuse the material furnished to it by the memory, thus producing completely new compounds, in the same way as chemistry operates with unknown elements. The imagination becomes all the more fertile when enriched by a cultivated memory, which places at its disposal a greater number of varied and precise elements. Thus it can be established that the cultivation of a pictorial memory, while strengthening and serving the imagination, undoubtedly favours artistic composition.' This practice of relying to a great extent on memory accorded with Whistler's own ideas; and Henri Focillon[1] even considered that by assimilating Lecoq de Boisbaudran's thesis, in which an ideal element linked the aesthetic of representation with that of suggestion, Whistler facilitated his own later acceptance of the principles of Japanese art.

But all this lay in the future. At this stage, Whistler was primarily a realist, intent on observing local life. It was typical of his flair for the significant currents of the hour and of his sense of timing that he should have turned to graphic art; this, at the very moment when the 'Etching Revival', as it was termed, was about to start. His understanding of, and affinity with, the realist attitude were brilliantly displayed in his first set of etchings—*Twelve Etchings from Nature*, which is generally, but incorrectly, termed 'The French Set'. These were the outcome of a walking tour of Northern France, Luxembourg and the Rhineland, which he had made with his friend and fellow student Ernest Delaunoy in 1858. Already, when employed by the Coastal Geodetic Survey in Washington, he had tried his hand at etching and earlier (as already pointed out) he executed two lithographs, but nothing he did then really foreshadowed the mastery displayed in these, his first formal etchings. Fortunately for him, they were printed by Auguste Delâtre, the most distinguished printer of etchings of the day, who had worked for Charles Meryon. Whistler probably never met this etcher whose work he despised, but he would almost certainly have seen his famous series of twenty-two etchings, *Eaux-Fortes sur Paris*, which were issued between 1850–1 and which included prints like *La Rue des Mauvais Garçons* or *L'Arche du Pont Notre Dame*.

On the other hand, Whistler seems to have examined the work of Charles Jacque, a member of the Barbizon school, and telling similarities have been detected,[2] with good reason, between Jacque's *Recureuse* and Whistler's *La Marchande de Moutarde* and between his *Ma Petite Fille* and Whistler's *Annie Haden seated*, which, however, is later in date than 'The French Set'. *La Marchande de Moutarde*

---

[1] See 'L'estampe japonaise et la Peinture en l'Occident dans la seconde moitié du XIXième siècle' in *Actes du Congrès de l'Histoire de l'Art (1921)*, 1923, Vol. I, pp. 367–76 and *La Peinture au XIX et XX Siècles*, 1928, p. 162.

[2] James Laver, *Whistler* (2nd edition), 1951, pp. 49–50.

and *La Vieille aux Loques* also suggest an awareness of Bonvin's paintings, while the charming naturalism of *En Plein Soleil* is akin to that found in Courbet's pictures. Doubtless he was aware of the Dutch seventeenth-century school and echoes of the intimate shadowy interiors painted by Rembrandt and Pieter de Hooch are discernible in a remarkable and atmospheric etching like *The Kitchen*.

It is natural for a young and alert artist to look around him in this way; but Whistler's dependence on the example of his predecessors and contemporaries did not hamper the emergence of his own personal and sensitive feelings. His application of the realist approach was by no means doctrinaire; *The Old Farm* and the *Street at Saverne* are touched with a romantic spirit. The first has something of the picturesque character associated with the sketches of architecture popular in the early nineteenth century. The second is more individual and of significance for his later work; the single figure picked out by a shaft of artificial light in a deserted street offers a foretaste of that silent and poetical mood which the artist was to explore so effectively in subsequent years. This print alone suffices to demonstrate his swift mastery of the medium. His originality is equally well shown in the tender (and exceedingly rare) etching of *Gretchen at Heidelberg* (p. 25): particularly daring is the treatment of the areas of shadow, worked out by means of subtle hatchings, which anticipate the technique of his drawings.

In the 1850s Whistler's talents were more effectively displayed in his etchings than in his paintings. Few pictures remain from the early years and their chronological sequence is by no means easy to work out. But it would seem as if the first picture of any merit he painted at this time—while still very much a student—was *La Mère Gérard*, of which three versions exist; of these the best known is that once belonging to the poet Swinburne, which was recently with Messrs Knoedler. This straightforward realistic portrait is obviously connected with his etching of the same woman in 'The French Set'. His second principal picture was the *Self Portrait* (Fig. 1) in the Freer Gallery, Washington, which acknowledges a vague debt to Rembrandt. Two other works, which may date either from this phase, before he had met Fantin-Latour and Legros, or just after he had done so, are the *Old Peasant smoking a Pipe* in the Louvre, which, however, bears a sort of similarity to Courbet's self-portraits and is certainly in the realistic manner, and the rather haunting *Peasant Woman* in the University of Glasgow's collection, which already betrays a sympathy for the inner life of the sitter, later such a feature of his mature portrait style.

His blossoming out as a painter occurred once he was in touch with the circle centred on Courbet. One should stress, however, that his prints indicate an evident awareness on Whistler's part of the new artistic movement before the two men actually met. Whistler himself, with the licence of reminiscence, claimed that in these days he was 'a surprising youth, suddenly appearing in the midst of the French students from no one knew where, with my *mère Gérard* and the *Piano*

Picture for introduction, and making friends with Fantin and Legros, who had already arrived, and Courbet, whom they were all raving about, and who was very kind to me'.[1]

The image he presents is attractive: that of the brilliant conquering young artist, but it is not altogether accurate—in one important particular. Whereas he had certainly painted *La Mère Gérard* before meeting Fantin-Latour, he only began work on *At the Piano* (Fig. 2), in the Cincinnati Art Museum, in November,

GRETCHEN AT HEIDELBERG
Etching, 8 × 6⅛ in. Signed 'Whistler'.
One of 'The French Set', 1858.
Lessing Rosenwald Collection, National
Gallery, Washington.

1858—a month after he had come across him in the Louvre where they were both copying the same picture. The two men obviously took an immediate liking to each other and in the evening of the same day, the young French painter introduced Whistler to several of his friends, members of a circle which included Legros, Carolus-Duran and Astruc: there Whistler, so the story runs, produced 'The French Set'—his passport to the world of the Realists.[2]

This meeting must have still further stimulated his interest in contemporary

[1] Pennell, I, p. 68.

[2] In a letter of 26th June, 1859, to Whistler talking about his etchings, Fantin-Latour said, *vous savez que j'ai été leur premier amateur, celui qui les a comprises au Café Voltaire.* University of Glasgow.

art; it doubtless accounts for the technical accomplishment and greater understanding of pictorial values shown in *At the Piano* (Fig. 2). For a start he chose
a modern subject, an interior representing his half-sister Deborah Haden and her
daughter, Annie (later Mrs Charles Thynne), and this is treated in a way which
would have appealed to a Dutch seventeenth-century painter or to Chardin whose
work, incidentally, was admired by one of his *avant-garde* friends, Bonvin. The
picture's harmonious style bears considerable resemblance to that of Fantin-
Latour's *The Artist's Sisters embroidering* in the City Art Museum, St Louis, and
to Degas's famous *Portrait of the Bellelei Family* in the Louvre, Paris, both of which
date from 1859, the year in which Whistler's own picture was painted. He had not
yet met Degas, whose painting, in any case, was executed in Florence, but he was
close to Fantin; and it would be interesting to determine which artist influenced
the other: unfortunately no firm evidence is available on this point.

All three pictures certainly reflect a mood of calm intimacy, with a more classical
note uppermost in Degas's, and they seem to constitute a moment of repose—
before the revolutionary outbreak of Impressionism. In Whistler's case, this
tranquil effect was achieved owing to the sparse and controlled design evident in
the relationships established between the lines made by the pictures on the wall
and the moulding of the dado, and by the balance presented by Mrs Haden's
dark dress and the white dress worn by her daughter; moreover, the red carpet is
toned in with the table-cloth. Many of Whistler's most characteristic pictures
derive from this prototype; it is one of those revealing paintings, which, at the very
inception of an artist's career, announces a subsequent development and contains
those elements which are to become absolutely his own.

Today, *At the Piano* seems innocuous enough, yet it was rejected at the Salon
of 1859, a fate also suffered by the pictures sent in by Fantin-Latour, Legros and
Ribot. Whistler's painting, as well as those by his three colleagues, so Fantin-
Latour stated,[1] were duly placed on view in a sort of private exhibition held at
Bonvin's studio, *son atelier Flamand*, as he called it, at 189 rue St Jacques, where,
the same witness recalled, Courbet 'was struck with Whistler's picture'.[2] Whistler
had now 'arrived', as far as the Paris *avant garde* was concerned; he had become so
close to Fantin-Latour and Legros that they established a little group on their
own—the *Société des Trois* as they called it—which existed mainly as a sort of mutual
protection and admiration society; however, broadly speaking, at this time all
subscribed to similar aesthetic ideals. A delightful memento of Whistler's friendship
with Fantin-Latour in these early days is provided by the drawing, in the Louvre,
of the Frenchman working in bed, dressed, with his hat on, owing to the cold. This
was done in December, 1859, and is reproduced on page. 29.

Some idea of the degree of intimacy which bound the two men can be gained
from a letter which Whistler wrote to Fantin-Latour in 1864 when the French

---

[1] Pennell, I, p. 75.   [2] Pennell, I, p. 25.

artist's famous *Hommage à Delacroix* (Louvre) was being shown in the Salon. In this he spoke of their 'long evening chats', and, as he said, 'I like to think that we are necessary to each other as we enjoy that real exchange of sympathies which we can't find with others. At least I've never had entire confidence in the sympathy of anybody except yourself.'[1]

Although *At the Piano* was excluded from the Paris Salon, Whistler was luckier when he sent it to the Royal Academy in 1860, and its acceptance indicates that on occasions the London hanging committee could prove more liberal than its Paris counterpart. It is, in fact, quite clear that with this picture the artist achieved a certain success, and the Academician John Phillip, who specialised in painting Spanish subject-pictures, actually bought it for £30. Moreover, the veteran Thackeray looked at it with real delight and appreciation,[2] George Boughton admired it,[3] while Millais told the young painter: 'I never flatter, but I will say that your picture is the finest piece of colour that has been on the walls of the Royal Academy for many years.'[4]

The press also mentioned the picture. The *Daily Telegraph*'s critic[5] was caustic enough, dubbing it 'an eccentric uncouth, smudgy, phantom-like picture of a lady at the pianoforte, with a ghostly looking child in a white frock looking on', but his colleague on the *Athenaeum* was more amiable. This writer, who also praised the etchings (hung in the Octagon Room), declared that 'despite a recklessly bold manner and sketchiness of the wildest and roughest kind', the picture possesses 'a genuine feeling for colour and a splendid power of composition and design, which evince a just appreciation of nature, very rare among artists'. 'If', he went on, 'the observer will look for a little while at this singular production, he will perceive that it opens out just as a stereoscopic view will—an excellent quality due to the artist's feeling for atmosphere and judicious gradations of light.' These press comments, as the Pennells correctly observed,[6] stress that Whistler was 'always noticed, both praised and blamed, never ignored, after 1859'. During his career, indeed, Whistler received numerous letters of congratulation from fellow artists; and there was no reason for him to feel quite so persecuted and neglected as he often chose to make out.

The rather friendly reception which *At the Piano* received at the Royal Academy doubtless contributed to Whistler's decision to spend more time in London. There

[1] This quotation is from the large group of letters to Fantin-Latour in the Library of Congress, Washington. Extracts from these were printed by L. Bénédite in 'Artistes Contemporains: Whistler' in *Gazette des Beaux Arts*, xxxiii (1905), pp. 403–10 and 496–511 and xxxiv (1905), pp. 142–58 and 231–46.

[2] Pennell, I, pp. 82–3.   [3] Pennell, I, p. 83.

[4] Cited by George du Maurier in a letter of May, 1860; see *The Young George du Maurier*, 1951, p. 4. Millais's own painting, *Portrait of Mrs James Wyatt and her daughter Susan*, 1849, is almost a precursor of Whistler's intimate style.

[5] Both this quotation and that from *The Athenaeum* are found in Pennell, I, p. 83.

[6] Op. cit., p. 83.

was much to attract him in London; for one thing, he could stay with his half-sister, Deborah, and her husband, the surgeon and etcher Seymour Haden, in their comfortable home in Sloane Street, and the quiet intimate atmosphere of this haven, doubtless very welcome after the more primitive conditions of the Quartier Latin, is suggested in his delicate etching *Reading by Lamplight*. Moreover, Whistler was shrewd enough to realise that he may have stood more chance of winning a position in London than in Paris. Once settled here his thoughts turned to his close friend Fantin-Latour whom he prevailed upon to cross over to London in the summer of 1859, where they both admired Millais's *The Vale of Rest*, which was shown in the Royal Academy in that year. The other member of the *Société des Trois*, Alphonse Legros, also came to London in 1863, where he remained for the rest of his life. How successful he was at the start appears from the well-known letter to Fantin-Latour in which Whistler urged him to come to England to make his fortune: 'Alphonse (Legros) has only to put brush on canvas to make 1000 francs, never less than 800 francs. It's the same for me. In the space of three or four weeks, he has made nearly 8000 francs.'[1] In the same year, he emphasised that more than ever they would form the *Société des Trois*: 'we will make our fortune and quickly, for you know that I will do my duty—and to support each other is to support ourselves'.[1] Almost from the start, Whistler considered himself as a sort of gang leader; a rôle repeated in later years.

The artistic situation in mid-nineteenth-century England was by no means bleak. A new force had been generated by the Pre-Raphaelites, who had come to the fore in the 1850s; moreover, during the first decade of Whistler's residence in England, considerable efforts were made, both in the capital and the provinces, to disseminate a knowledge of art. Whistler's own decision to settle here possibly reflects his awareness of this developing concern for the arts; and he was by no means uninterested in what he saw in England. Many British painters took modern themes for their pictures and a number of 'realistic' works by well-known men like W. R. Frith (whom Whistler admired in the early days) and Ford Madox Brown, as well as less familiar artists like Alfred Elmore, date from this period; thus Brown's *An English Autumn Afternoon* in the City Art Gallery, Birmingham, was painted in 1854, Frith's *The Railway Carriage* (Royal Holloway College, Egham) in 1862 and Elmore's *On the Brink*, in Mr A. N. L. Munby's collection, in 1865. Indeed, any survey of mid-Victorian genre painting emphasises the extent to which subject matter was derived from contemporary life.

Generally speaking, however, the emphasis was placed not so much on the pictorial qualities as on the sentimental and anecdotic implications of the theme; this was an attitude which had emerged in the 1840s when a painter and writer like Richard Redgrave hoped to use painting for moral and social purposes and thus

[1] To Fantin-Latour. Undated letter, 1863. Library of Congress, Washington.

I. THE COAST OF BRITTANY. Canvas (34⅜ x 46 in.). Signed and dated lower left, Whistler/1861. Exhibited at the Royal Academy in 1862 under the title of Alone with the Tide. This is the first of the artist's major works to treat of the sea, a favourite theme (Wadsworth Atheneum, Hartford, Connecticut).

4 THE THAMES IN ICE: THE
25TH DECEMBER, 1860.

Canvas, 29⅜ × 21¾ in. Signed
'Whistler'. Freer Gallery of Art,
Washington.

5 WAPPING.

Canvas, 28 × 40 in. Signed and
dated 1861, but not completed until
1864. Mr and Mrs John Hay
Whitney, New York.

6 SYMPHONY IN WHITE
NO. I: THE WHITE GIRL.

*Canvas, 84½ × 42½ in. Signed
and dated 1862. Exhibited at the
Salon des Refusés, 1863.
National Gallery of Art,
Washington.*

7 FUMETTE.

*Etching, 6¾ × 4¼ in. Signed
'Whistler'. One of 'The French
Set'. 1858. Messrs P. and D.
Colnaghi, London.*

strove to help the afflicted and distressed; in this respect, a comparison between this painter's *The Poor Teacher* in the Victoria and Albert Museum, London, which was shown at the Royal Academy in 1845, and *At the Piano* is instructive. It brings out the way in which Whistler took a genre scene, one susceptible of a moralistic interpretation, and preferred to stress its pictorial side. His reading of realism led him to emphasise the relevance of the properties of painting as such;

FANTIN-LATOUR WORKING IN BED
Chalk drawing, $9\frac{5}{8} \times 6\frac{1}{8}$ in. Inscribed and dated 1859. Cabinet des Dessins, Musée du Louvre, Paris.

and by doing so he collided with the generally accepted standards of contemporary taste.

The bane of English painting at this period, in fact, was a widespread pre-occupation with subjects of a sentimental character. Whistler himself gave a lively account of how the choice of subject matter preoccupied the painter, though doubtless, with this statement, as so often with him, his tongue was in his cheek: 'When I came to London I was received graciously by the painters. Then there was coldness, I could not understand. Artists locked themselves up in their studios—opened the doors only on the chain; if they met each other in the street they barely spoke. Models went round silent, with an air of mystery. When I asked one where she had been posing, she said: "To Frith and Watts and Tadema". "Golly! what a crew!" I said. "And that's just what they says when I told 'em I was a posing to you!" Then I found out the mystery: it was the moment of painting the Royal Academy picture. Each man was afraid his subject might be stolen. It was the great era of the subject. And, at last, on Varnishing Day, there was the subject in all its glory—wonderful. The British subject! Like a flash the inspiration came—the Inventor!—and in the Academy there you saw him: the familiar model— the soldier or the Italian—and there he sat, hands on knees, head bent, brows knit, eyes staring; in a corner, angels and cogwheels and things; close to him his wife, cold, ragged, the baby in her arms—he had failed! The story was told—it was clear as day—amazing!—the British subject. What.'[1]

As a true realist, he found his themes in the world around him. During his first years in London he was engaged in discovering and exploiting the local scene, coming across congenial motifs in Greenwich Park, where he made a number of charming etchings in 1858, and on the Thames, where he began work in the summer of that year. He was by no means the first nor the last artist to have responded to the appeal of the river: Claude de Jongh, Canaletto, William Marlow, Samuel Scott, Constable, Turner, Monet, Derain and Nicolas de Staël were all fascinated by its qualities of light and movement. Although familiar with London since his youth, Whistler, as a foreigner, must have been forcibly struck by the importance of this artery of a great commercial city and, consequently, by its relevance for his aims. His contemporary Gautier had described the Thames as taking a place in London similar to that of the Boulevards in Paris, as the principal line of circulation. 'The moving panorama (were his words) which ceaselessly occurs is something so novel and grand that one cannot tear oneself away from it.'[2]

In these years Whistler was attracted by the bustle and liveliness associated with the river and not, as later, by its poetical atmosphere. For him it was surely a vivid manifestation of the intensity of modern life; the true expression of modernity. His enjoyment of the river's potentialities is made clear in the sharply delineated prints which compose the famous *Thames Set* on which he began work in the summer of 1859. These show how he fastened on the individuality of the sailors and dockers, the activity of a busy seaport and the almost Dickensian character of existence down the river; and, as William Michael Rossetti observed, 'his etchings have always shown a marked propensity for shore-life, river-life, boat-life, barge-life— for everything which hints of old wharves, jetties, piers, rigging, bow-windows, overlooking reaches of the peopled stream and that class of hard-fisted, square-shouldered, solid and stolid faced men, in whom the odour of tar and of tobacco is equally incorporate'.[3] This is just the atmosphere pungently conveyed in prints

[1] Pennell, I, pp. 81–2.

[2] T. Gautier, 'Une Journée à Londres' in *Caprices et Zigzags*, 1852, p. 123.

[3] See *Fine Art, Chiefly Contemporary; Notices Re-Printed, with Revisions*, 1867, p. 272.

like the Thames *Warehouses* or the *Rotherhithe* (Fig. 11). Yet he did not pose his sitters, as it were, solely to gain the picturesque effect; on the contrary, they are blended in with their surroundings and in a number of prints like *Billingsgate* or the *Little Wapping* he was primarily concerned with rendering the structure of buildings or the impression made by bare masts with furled sails.

[Whistler's affinity with modern French painting was brought out in the remarkable *Thames in Ice* (Fig. 4) in the Freer Gallery, Washington, which was shown at the Royal Academy in 1862. For virtually the first time he may be seen really enjoying the atmospheric qualities of the Thames; and the treatment of the rather misty and indefinite outlines of the factories smoking away in the far-distance foreshadows that conception of space, as evocative of a mood, which was to characterise the Nocturnes.] The simplification apparent in it may have owed something to his experiences and experiments as an etcher. At this time, too, he started to work on the well-known *Wapping* (Fig. 5) in the collection of Mr and Mrs John Hay Whitney, New York; however, although this picture carries the date 1861, it was not completed until 1864 when it was exhibited at the Royal Academy.

During the 1860s, Whistler did not pursue one course alone; he was interested in a variety of themes which required, and duly received, different means of expression. It was an indication of his vitality and zest for experiment that this was so. In other words, he started in certain directions only virtually to abandon their exploitation once he found that they neither answered to his real needs nor reflected his principal preoccupations. His interest in realism was as keen as ever, but his growing concern with a tasteful arrangement of his subject matter, evident almost from the start in *At the Piano* (Fig. 2), was confirmed in one of his most important early pictures, the *Harmony in Green and Rose: The Music Room* (Fig. 3) in the Freer Gallery, Washington.

This is a straightforward interior, admirably painted, very light and cheerful in tone, with a dark red carpet, chintzy curtains, and green-grey wall paper. There is nothing enclosed nor stuffy about the picture as with so many Victorian interiors. In the same way as in *At the Piano*, considerable care was taken with the planning of the composition: thus the horizontal lines formed by the picture frames are used to bring out the vertical form of one of the main figures in the painting, Miss Boot with her graceful silhouette. The intense black of her riding habit, characteristically, is offset by the white dress of Annie Haden, who is placed under the light coming from an unseen window; while Mrs Haden's reflection is captured in the mirror. By these means, the sitters are rendered casually and an impression registered, though not, of course, in the Impressionist manner. The stance chosen for Miss Boot is especially interesting; it seems to anticipate that graceful *déhanchement* which the artist later fastened upon when he found it in Japanese prints and Tanagra figures; her actual pose bears a resemblance to that adopted by

Courbet in his portraits of women. A closer link with this master is afforded by the *Portrait of Luke Ionides* (Cyril Ionides collection, Sussex); this was commissioned by the sitter's father, the collector Alexander Ionides, after having seen *At the Piano* (Fig. 2) at the Royal Academy in 1860. However, Whistler's insight into character and his developing skill as a portraitist is most effectively seen in his prints—those of Annie Haden, Axenfeld, and Riault, the engraver.

Whistler, who could be both charming and adroit in society, was now enjoying a certain amount of personal success in London. His range of acquaintances, however, was still relatively narrow; but he was particularly well received by Anglo-Greek families like the Ionides and the Spartali. 'A more enchanting vagabond cannot be conceived' was the comment of George du Maurier,[1] who shared a studio with him for some time in the early 60s: 'He is in my opinion the grandest genius I ever met, a giant—considered besides, as a "wit", greater than either Hook or Sidney Smith, by those who have met those swells.' He certainly made a hit and, to quote the same witness,[2] 'Jemmy's bon mots, which are plentiful, are the finest things I ever heard; and nothing that I ever read of in Dickens or anywhere can equal his *amazing* power of anecdote.' This impression did not last; a year later Du Maurier was to lament that 'nothing is more fatiguing than an egotistical wit'.[3]

Another friend was Charles Keene, whose work Whistler admired and of whom he made a charming portrait drawing now in the National Gallery at Melbourne. Some of the drawings by these two men, especially their sketches of women, have much in common, but their paths were to diverge; nevertheless, Keene continued to admire Whistler's work and was especially enthusiastic about the Venetian pastels.[4] He was also on friendly terms with Edward Poynter and, according to Armstrong, his old friend from the Paris period, Whistler would paint still life in Poynter's studio in Grafton Street; however, none of these seem to have survived.[5]

During his Paris days, Whistler, as we have seen, had enjoyed a liaison with a grisette. On settling in London he formed another attachment—this time with an Irish girl, Joanna Heffernan. She was the daughter of a bohemian Irishman, who always spoke about Whistler as 'me son-in-law'. Jo served as the model for many of his finest early pictures, including *Wapping* (Fig. 5), in the collection of Mr and Mrs John Hay Whitney, New York, and the *Symphony in White No. 1: The White Girl* (Fig. 6), in the National Gallery, Washington; and, although a woman of small education, she seems to have been relatively intelligent and certainly charming. However, if Du Maurier is to be believed, she gave herself grand airs and the artist is said to have stood 'in mortal fear' of her; the same writer maintained

---

[1] Op. cit., p. 4. Letter of May, 1860.   [2] Op. cit., p. 11. Letter of June, 1860.
[3] Op. cit., p. 16. Letters of October, 1860.   [4] Derek Hudson, *Charles Keene*, 1947, p. 47.
[5] Op. cit., p. 199. A still life, 'The Green Umbrella', attributed to Whistler, was sold at Christie's as Lot 21, 22nd June, 1962 (reproduced), from the collection of William Rolfe, Jr. and Stephen Juvelis.

(in 1864) that she was 'an awful tie'.[1] Nevertheless, although Whistler arranged for her to move out of his house when his mother arrived from America, he does seem to have quarrelled with his brother-in-law, Haden, on her account. She remained his mistress until sometime in the late 1860s or early 1870s, when she was replaced by the more elegant Maud Franklin (Fig. 47), who was in command until his marriage to Mrs Godwin (Fig. 52).

[1] Op. cit., p. 227. Letter of February, 1864. However, in 1866 the artist wrote a will in her favour.

❧ TWO ❧

Realist or Pre-Raphaelite

FOR Whistler, an expatriate, with one foot in Paris and the other in London, the claims of both capitals and of their advanced artistic movements were mutually seductive. Yet during the 1860s he was gradually to swing in the direction of England, sharing in certain intellectual and artistic problems which were current here, but his involvement was never so deep as to make him forget his French affiliations. In fact, several of his most interesting and vital works were done in France which he and Jo Heffernan visited on various occasions; in 1861, for instance, they stayed in the Boulevard des Batignolles, Montmartre. One side of his nature made him very much an *avant garde* painter in the French manner and, at this stage, the experimentalism of his style is especially revealed in the *Coast of Brittany* (Plate I) in the Wadsworth Atheneum, Hartford, Connecticut. This was painted in Brittany in September, 1861, and favourably received at the Royal Academy in the following year, possibly owing to its title 'Alone with the Tide'. By going to Brittany, Whistler revealed his alertness to new trends because this region had already attracted some of the French Realists, among them Bonvin; writing from Dinard some eight years before, this painter had expressed his delight at finding 'sea and rocks everywhere; and a beautiful carpet of sand under one's feet'.[1]

The rugged nature of the Brittany coast cast its spell on Whistler. The little peasant girl in the composition bears some resemblance to the type of model favoured by his friend Legros and her costume is akin to those worn by the figures in typical Pont-Aven pictures of the 1880s. Yet obviously his chief aim was to evoke the desolate atmosphere of the beach. His interest in painting the sparse structure of the rocks foreshadows an approach favoured by Daubigny, whose austere rocky coast scenes, however, date only from 1865; not that this painter was in any way influenced by Whistler. On the other hand, Whistler himself presumably remembered Courbet when painting this picture; its theme and treatment seem to presuppose some awareness on his part of this artist's

[1] A letter of 28th August, 1853 (from Dinard) to Borie; see Etienne Moreau-Nélaton, *Bonvin raconté par lui même*, 1927, p. 43.

34

lovely *Seashore at Palavas*, dating from 1853–4, in the Musée Fabre at Montpellier. But the traffic between the two men was by no means one way only; and Whistler's *The Blue Wave* (Fig. 8), in the Hill-Stead Museum, Farmington, Conn., painted when he was staying on the coast at Guéthary, between Biarritz and St Jean de Luz, in the autumn of 1862, implies that he actually anticipated Courbet in depicting a broken wave, a motif this artist himself used only some years later, when working at Trouville, Deauville and, above all, at Etrétat.

This stay in the Basses-Pyrénées, which was intended as a prelude to moving on to Madrid, greatly contributed to Whistler's artistic evolution and to deepening his conception of realism. He was concerned to discover a way of using paint sketchily and of catching the mood of a scene and its immediate impression; and he told his customary confidant Fantin-Latour: 'In any case, these pictures painted out of doors after nature, *en plein air*, cannot be anything else than large sketches; a bit of floating drapery, a wave, a cloud, it's there for a moment, then it disappears and the true tone has to be caught in flight just as one shoots a flying bird. But the public demands finished works.'[1] However, his time was by no means comfortable, and at Brittany he complained bitterly to Fantin-Latour about the ceaseless rain. Yet he did start a figure composition, representing Jo 'quite clear and in rose' next to an old woman in black, a sailor with a red shirt, and 'waves that are superb (in nature); breakers so solid that they seem carved in stone'. And he provided his friend with a sketch of it in the letter. However, as he told him, 'I am almost demoralised by these lost days—and these weeks which pass by. Now I am compelled to abandon my picture until next year. I will leave my canvas here and return to finish it. Yes, *mon cher*, you are right—painting after nature, this ought to be done at home.'

During the early 1860s, Whistler's reputation with the French public—the *avant garde* public rather—was growing, partly owing to his etchings. His brilliance in this medium was unquestionable; it may be seen not only in the 'Thames Set', but in such well observed realistic scenes as the *Soupe à Trois Sous* (p. 39, executed in Paris), *The Forge* (which he did at Perros-Guirec in Brittany in 1861) and the dramatic *The Miser*, with its echo of an early Rembrandt; according to the artist himself, this represented a room in a farm at Maladrie. He was in contact with some of his French colleagues who were fascinated by this medium, and in 1862 he became a member of the newly formed *Société des Aquafortistes* which was to change its name and turn into *L'Illustration Nouvelle* in 1868. In the summer of 1862, as well, the 'Thames Set' of etchings was exhibited at Martinet's Gallery in Paris where Baudelaire, with customary acumen, praised them: they were, he said, '*merveilleux fouillis d'agrès, de vergues, de cordages; chaos de brumes, de fourneaux*

[1] This and the following two quotations come from a group of undated letters, written from the Maison de la Croix, chez Monsieur Louis Daguerre, Guéthary. They are in the Library of Congress, Washington.

et de fumées tire-bouchonnées; poésie profonde et compliquée d'une vaste capitale'.[1]
It was typical of Baudelaire's sensitivity that he should have grasped Whistler's
attempt to convey the atmospheric effects of a great city; not that the painter was
entirely satisfied with the critic's observations, complaining to Fantin-Latour that
'Baudelaire waxes poetical about the Thames but says nothing about my etchings
themselves'.[2]

His rôle as a member of the French modern movement was consolidated in
1863 when his *Symphony in White No. 1: The White Girl* (Fig. 6), in the National
Gallery, Washington, was rejected at the official Salon, but exhibited at the
Salon des Refusés, established by Napoleon III. This picture had been
rejected at the Royal Academy in 1862, but shown at Mathew Morgan's gallery,
14 Berners Street, London, in the summer of that year. It was started in the winter
of 1861 and the model was Jo. Its appearance at the Salon des Refusés aroused
immediate controversy; and some years later Zola recalled in his novel, *L'Œuvre*,
the hysterical crowds gathered in front of the picture. P. G. Hamerton, the
English art critic, described too how parties would stand and look at it 'struck
with amazement. This for two or three seconds, then they always looked at each
other and laughed.'[3] Needless to say, he joined in the merriment.

With the Paris élite, the picture scored a triumph. In a letter written at six
in the evening after leaving the exhibition, Fantin-Latour reported to the artist:
'Now you are famous. Your picture is very well hung. You have won a great
success. We find the whites excellent; they are superb, and at a distance (that's the
real test) they look first class. Courbet calls your picture an apparition, with a
spiritual content; (this annoys him); he says it's good; this will annoy someone who
does badly. Baudelaire finds it charming, charming, exquisite, absolutely delicate,
as he says. Legros, Manet, Bracquemond, de Balleroy and myself; we all think it
admirable.'[4] Praise also came from Thoré-Bürger,[5] one of the most intelligent critics
of the time, who noted that Whistler's picture occasioned the greatest comment in
the Salon, and this incidentally in an exhibition which included Manet's *Le
Dejeuner sur L'Herbe*, now in the Louvre, Paris, and *Mlle V (Victorine Meurent)
en costume*, in the Metropolitan Museum, New York.

For one critic, at any rate, the picture was something more than a study in
white; in Castagnary's view, it possessed an allegorical significance. For him it

---

[1] The first version of this article appeared in the *Revue Anecdotique*, 2nd April, 1862, and a later, fuller
one in *Le Boulevard*, 14th September, 1862: see Baudelaire, *Oeuvres*, 2 vols. (edition Pléiade), ed. Y-G
Le Dantec, 1938, Vol. 2, p. 292.

[2] Letter from Guéthary, autumn, 1862. Library of Congress, Washington.

[3] In the *Fine Arts Quarterly*, cited by Pennell, I, p. 102.

[4] To Whistler, Letter of (May) 1863, University of Glasgow.

[5] *Salons de W. Bürger*, I. p. 414 'Le Salon de 1863' cited by J. C. Sloane, *French Painting Between the
Past and the Present*, 1951, p. 186.

8 THE BLUE WAVE: BIARRITZ.
Canvas, 24½ × 34 in. Signed 'Whistler'. 1862. Hill-Stead Museum, Farmington, Conn.

9 BATTERSEA REACH.
Canvas, 20 × 30 in. About 1863–64. Corcoran Gallery of Art, Washington.

10 HARMONY IN GREY: CHELSEA IN IC

*Canvas, $17\frac{1}{2} \times 24$ in. About 1864. Priva
Collection, London.*

11 ROTHERHITHE (WAPPING).

*Etching, $10\frac{1}{4} \times 7\frac{3}{4}$ in. Signed
'Whistler 1860'. One of 'The Thames
Set', 1871. Corcoran Gallery of Art, Washington.*

represented a young woman on the morning after her bridal night—this was just the sort of theme which fascinated many people at this time. He wrote in his review, '"what have you wanted to do?" I asked the strange painter, whose fantastic etchings I alone had previously admired. "A *tour de force* of your craft as a painter, consisting of dashing off whites on whites? Permit me not to believe it. Let me see in your work something loftier, *The Bride's Tomorrow*, that troubling moment when the young woman questions herself and is astonished at no longer recognising in herself the virginity of the night before" ';[1] the comparison he then made with Greuze's *La Cruche cassée* seems almost inevitable. In a sense, one may sympathise with Castagnary and understand what he wished to imply; although the artist concentrated on facing up to the pictorial problems involved in the composition—the posing of a full-length figure against a neutral background offset by the richer hues found in the rug at her feet—and managed to achieve his aims, the picture's final impression is of the girl's melancholy; as Théodore Duret said 'she is painted like a vision, which appears not to everybody but to a poet'.[2] The picture's bold handling is impressive: thus the strokes of blue paint on the rug are related to the Impressionist technique and in the background—a hanging curtain—the tones are varied and the contrasts secured by means of the palette knife.

Whistler was never a literary artist in the accepted sense of the term—such an outlook was quite opposed to his most cherished beliefs—but his own words about *Wapping* (Fig. 5) emphasise that, in certain pictures, his ambition was to provide an 'expression'. The *Symphony in White No. 1: The White Girl* takes on a special and highly important part in his development; it was hung among the most radical works then being painted in Paris; it excited his French friends; but it was also an intimation that realism was not to hold him. The extent to which he was influenced by his surroundings and imbibed the contemporary views of the English *avant garde* (which was very different from its French counterpart) remains a moot point; but residence in England brought Whistler close in spirit to the Pre-Raphaelites, whose works he could have seen on exhibition and in the houses or studios of his friends. With her auburn hair, her languid look and her touch of sadness, *The White Girl* is partly a Pre-Raphaelite picture. Whistler's highly receptive nature to complex moods helps to explain his response to the Pre-Raphaelites, just as in his later pictures it explains his drawing close to the Symbolists.

Nevertheless, one has to avoid leaping to conclusions about the way in which such influences actually worked. It would be tempting to argue that, prior to

[1] In 'Le Salon des refusés', *Salons, 1857–1870*, 2 vols. Preface by Eugène Spuller, 1892, Vol. I, p. 179, cited by J. C. Sloane, op. cit., p. 186, note 37.

[2] *Histoire de J. McN. Whistler et de son Oeuvre*, 1904, p. 22. (An English edition was published in 1917.)

painting his own picture, he had seen Rossetti's *Ecce Ancilla Domini* (National Gallery, London) of 1849–53, which F. M. Hueffer appropriately once termed 'a symphony in white', but it was unlikely that he did so; it was painted before he came over to London from Paris and acquired by a Belfast collector, the shipping agent McCracken, who presumably took it to Ireland with him. It is a question rather of affinities between the two artists; so that a work like Rossetti's *Beata Beatrix* (National Gallery, London), which was finished in 1863 and symbolises a memory of the dead Elizabeth Siddal, seems to belong to the same world as *The White Girl*, which depicts the more vital Jo. The drawings and illustrations by both men—notably those Whistler contributed to the press[1]—are also allied; indeed the American's are markedly Pre-Raphaelite in mood and technique. Yet how much bolder he could prove than Rossetti is emphasised by the black chalk drawing (in the Lessing Rosenwald Collection, National Gallery of Art, Washington) that he made for the etching *Weary*, in which the strong hatchings and the formal qualities of the figure may be related to Millet's drawings and even to Seurat's.

Whistler and Rossetti[2] were to meet only in the summer of 1862—shortly after *The White Girl* had been started; their relations became closer when Whistler moved to No. 7 Lindsey Row, Chelsea (now 101 Cheyne Walk), early in 1863; this was very near 'Tudor House' where Rossetti had gone to live in the previous autumn. Whistler was just the man to fit into the rather Bohemian set which surrounded Rossetti and which included Meredith and Swinburne, both of whom stayed at Tudor House for a year. These were the sort of creative people whose outlook and behaviour were not really dissimilar from those of his Parisian friends; their intellectual and artistic sympathies were certainly broader and keener than those of a Du Maurier or a Thomas Armstrong. Whistler and Swinburne became especially close; the poet would style Whistler in his letters as *mon père*, signing them most affectionately.[3] Their mutual interest in modern French literature probably helped to bring them together and in February, 1863, Fantin-Latour asked Whistler to tell the poet that 'Baudelaire had read his article

---

[1] E.g. four illustrations in *Once a Week* and two in *Good Words:* the commission for those in *Once a Week* were arranged by the Brothers Dalziel: see Pennell, I, p. 99.

[2] In later years, Whistler recalled his fellow artist with sympathy, stating in the draft autobiography (University of Glasgow) 'Poor Rossetti. A Prince among his fellows. Well do I remember with strong affection the barbaric court in which he reigned with the joyous simple ingenuous superiority as he throned it in Chelsea.' For his part Rossetti declared: 'Alas for Jimmy Whistler! What harbour of refuge now, unless to turn Fire King at Cremorne?—And Cremorne itself is no more! A Nocturne Andante in the direction of the Sandwich Islands, or some country where tattooing pure and simple is the national school of Art, can now alone avert the long-impending arrangement in Black and White.' The tone is ironical, to say the least, of this unpublished letter by Rossetti to William Davies when Whistler's bankruptcy threatened, cited by Francis Bickley, *The Pre-Raphaelite Comedy*, 1932, p. 58.

[3] See *The Swinburne Letters*, 1959, ed. Cecil Y. Lang, Vol. I. 1854–69, pp. 118–20.

with great enjoyment and that his verses, August, had seemed to him to be excellent'.[1] They helped each other too. Swinburne, for example, met Manet through Whistler's good offices and, on his side, Swinburne endeavoured to arrange for Ruskin to see his friend's paintings, telling him that 'Whistler was the first critic who so far overpraised my verse as to rank it above his own painting. I stood up against him for himself, and well, of course, against all others.'[2] As they knew

SOUPE À TROIS SOUS
Etching, 5⅞ × 8⅞ in. *Signed 'Whistler'. British Museum, London.*

each other so closely, can we be surprised that Whistler's brilliant drypoint of the poet (originally destined for the second edition of *Atalanta*) should seem to hint at the poet's curious nature; Whistler could prove a sharp observer of human foibles, if he wanted.

Swinburne found much to fascinate him in Whistler's painting in the 1860s and he wrote fulsomely about it. Moreover, the *Symphony in White No. 2: The Little White Girl* (Fig. 12, Tate Gallery, London), inspired the delightful poem, 'Before the Mirror,' of which stanzas four to six are printed here:

[1] In the University of Glasgow.
[2] Letter of 1st February (?), 1866, op. cit., I, p. 130.

Come snow, come wind or thunder,
High up in air,
I watch my face, and wonder
At my bright hair;
Nought else exalts or grieves
The rose at heart, that heaves
With love of her own leaves and lips that pair.

She knows not love that kissed her
She knows not where.
Art thou the ghost, my sister,
White sister there,
Am I the ghost, who knows?
My hand, a fallen rose,
Lies snow-white on white snow, and takes no care.

I cannot see what pleasures
Or what pains were;
What pale new loves and treasures
New years will bear;
What beam will fall, what shower,
What grief or joy for dower;
But one thing knows the flower—the flower is fair.

Whistler admired these lines so greatly that he had them printed on gold paper and pasted to the frame; two stanzas, Nos. 4 and 6, appeared in the exhibition catalogue. Some years later, Swinburne explained that the idea for the poem was 'entirely and only suggested to me by the picture, where I found at once the metaphor of the rose, and the notion of sad and glad mystery in the face languidly contemplative of its own phantom and all other things seen by their phantoms'.[1]

The picture itself is tinged with a dreaminess which makes of the earthy and voluptuous Jo (as she appeared, for instance, to Courbet) a creature imbued with the rather wan nostalgia of the mid-century romantics. Evidently one side of the artist's nature inclined him towards the cultivation of that type of ideal feminine beauty which captivated many contemporary painters and writers. He, too, could delight in paying homage to the aesthete's ideal of feminine beauty, at any rate in his art. This type of woman, associated with the craze for 'the stunner' in mid-Victorian circles, was admired just because she seemed almost unattainable —a sort of perpetual *demi-vierge*, one is almost inclined to feel. She was an Anglo-

---

[1] Letter of 2nd April, 1865, op. cit., pp. 118–20. For a contrary view, see T. Earle Welby, *The Victorian Romantics, 1850–1870*, 1929, pp. 52–7.

Saxon version of the Medusa figure, which so tantalised the French *fin de siècle*; however, like a Kate Greenaway illustration, the English version has an implicit innocence!

Fortunately for Whistler, however, he was spared the entanglements—Elizabeth Siddal, Fanny Cornforth and Janey Morris—which beset and tormented his friend Rossetti; Whistler's relationship with his mistresses seems to have been mainly complicated by that vexed problem of knowing how and when to break off! Nevertheless, by painting Jo in this way, not once, but on several occasions, he revealed the close ties which linked his vision with the Pre-Raphaelite outlook and with the aesthetic revolt against Victorian principles; also, it provides a source for that preoccupation with adolescence and with the ideal of a pure, unspotted young girl, which in his later years attracted him so strongly.

Although tempted by the aestheticism associated with the Pre-Raphaelites, Whistler did not altogether give up his realist position. One has constantly to remember that the particular character of his talent permitted him to explore within the same period a number of dissimilar styles, and each of these answered to different preoccupations. And by going to live in Chelsea he was not only close to Rossetti, he was near the Thames, which he adored as much as did his friend. The etchings and a picture like the *Thames in Ice* (Fig. 4) demonstrate the river's growing hold on him and, increasingly, he was seduced by the suggestive qualities of its atmosphere, even if he still took as his theme a special event; this was the case with the *Last of Old Westminster*, in the Museum of Fine Arts, Boston. This picture was painted in 1862 from the windows of Arthur Severn's brother's rooms in Manchester Buildings (the present site of Scotland Yard). The description of his methods of work underlines his intense concentration on the study of the motif. 'It was the piles with their rich colour and delightful confusion that took his fancy, not the bridge, which hardly showed. He would look steadily at a pile for some time, then mix up the colour, then holding his brush quite at the end, with no mahlstick, make a downward stroke and the pile was done. I remember once his looking very carefully at a hansom cab that had pulled up for some purpose on the bridge, and in a few strokes he got the look of it perfectly. He was a long time over the picture, sometimes coming only once a week, and we got rather tired of it.'[1]

Nevertheless, the final result is not laboured; it is spontaneous and fresh: and the liquid rapid technique harks back to that in the *Thames in Ice* (Fig. 4); however, the brush strokes are not so broad as in that work. His colours include russet, green, mauve, yellow, beside his usual greys and blacks. Severn's account of Whistler's execution is especially interesting; it underlines his determination to record an impression, but one filtered by the memory; to this extent, he was relatively close to certain experiments made by his French colleagues, not that he

[1] Pennell, I, p. 101.

attempted to dissolve light in the impressionist manner. In any event, this procedure only occurred later on. This picture is obviously connected with the *Brown and Silver: Old Battersea Bridge* (Addison Gallery of American Art, Andover) and the *Grey and Silver: Old Battersea Reach* (Art Institute, Chicago); both of these provide evidence of his increasing delight in manipulating perspective and his love for a faint and misty far-distance. The recessions are gently, almost imperceptibly registered, and in *Old Battersea Bridge* touches of green and brown are used to intensify the pervasive brown tonality, while monotony is avoided by the vivaciously handled group of fishermen in the foreground; these, quite fortuitously, recall analogous figures in Vernet's Italian scenes, and anticipate the type of figure found in Monet's pictures of the late 1860s. Here, too, may be discerned some of those elements which were later synthesised and transposed into the more poetical language of his Nocturnes—the little boat with the white sail or the barges which take on the appearance of dhows.

It was around this time, when he was living at Lindsey Row, as he himself later stated, that he painted the extraordinarily vivacious *Battersea Reach* (Fig. 9), in the Corcoran Gallery, Washington; in this work his growing desire to paint with liquid colours was matched by a care for rich tonalities—especially the russet tones so apparent in this canvas. It was, the artist declared, painted 'on a brilliant autumn evening',[1] and the picture remained one of his favourites.

His experiments with, and growing interest in, simplification were manifest in the *Harmony in Grey: Chelsea in Ice* (Fig. 10), in an English private collection, which may be dated to 1864 and is probably one of the two pictures described by the artist's mother. This admirable old lady, who had set up house with her son in 1863, related how 'During a very sharp frost, of a few days, I think for two days, ice was passing as we looked out upon the Thames. He could not resist painting, while I was shivering at the open window, two sketches which all say are most effective; one takes in the bridge. Of course they are not finished; he could not leave his Oriental paintings.'[2] In this canvas, the white paint dragged across the surface bears a distinct resemblance to the liquid tonalities found in the sketch for *Rose and Silver: La Princesse du Pays de la Porcelaine* of about 1863–4 (now in the Worcester Art Museum, Massachusetts), while the figures leaning nonchalantly on the parapet recall those in the earlier pictures of the Thames. The *Harmony in Grey* illustrates the way in which Whistler was in the process of combining a view of an observed scene with the invocation of a mood; as such, it remains one of the most poetical of his earlier paintings.

During these years, 1861–4, he was engaged on *Wapping* (Fig. 5) which he

[1] Letter of 17th August, 1893, in the possession of the Corcoran Gallery, Washington.
[2] In a letter of 10th February, 1864; see 'The Lady of the Portrait: Letters of Whistler's Mother' in *The Atlantic Monthly*, cxxxvi (1925), pp. 318–28. I owe this reference to Mr McLaren Young who is inclined, however, to date the painting rather later.

evidently intended to be an important work—a sort of subject picture. It was painted from an inn, the Angel, on the waterside at Cherry Gardens, which is apparently the same site from which he painted the *Thames in Ice*; the balcony shown in the picture is identical with that in the etching *Rotherhithe* (Fig. 11), though the view is different. The actual execution of the work caused him considerable difficulties, and he seems to have painted it at least three times. It carries the date 1861, but this must refer to the start of the picture as one of the main figures is Legros, who settled in London in 1863. It is possibly significant that in one of the three sketches for this canvas (one of which is on the leaf of his passport, the other two appear in a letter to Fantin-Latour[1]) the main male figure is shown without a beard—and Legros was heavily bearded. This letter, which would seem to date from around 1863, shows that Whistler had not yet decided on the actual arrangement of the figures; only the idea for the picture is sketched out, not its final appearance. He also introduced Jo into the picture, while the Pennells suggested[2] that the figure on the right was a workman from Greaves's ship-building firm in Chelsea, but no firm evidence exists on this point. Although telling Fantin-Latour that the picture still needed repainting, he was sufficiently satisfied with the result at this stage to report triumphantly: 'Finally, I've managed to give it an *expression*. Shut up, dear fellow, a real expression —such as you've never seen. It's made out of a red that's not golden but copper-coloured—everything one dreams about a Venetian girl. A white yellow skin or, golden, if you like. And with this famous expression I've just mentioned, she has the air of saying to her sailor: "That's all very well, *mon vieux*, but I've seen others." She winks as if making fun at him. This I've painted *contre jour* and consequently in half tones, which are frightfully hard to catch. However, I think I shall repaint it. For goodness sake, don't let on to Courbet about it.'

What Whistler precisely meant by his use of the term 'expression' is by no means clear; presumably he was trying to represent a scene which could be interpreted in the way outlined to Fantin-Latour—as a sort of conversation piece. The reference to Courbet is intriguing; it anticipates his reaction against this artist, described in his long communication to Fantin-Latour of 1867, and it affords another illustration of his rather ambivalent attitude to Courbet, whose demonstrable influence on his work he later went out of his way to denigrate. In this picture, the handling of Legros's head does suggest some awareness of this artist; however, it is as well to remember that any head with bearded features, especially if the sitter happens to be an artist, is apt to recall his work. As a whole, the composition and the treatment are not particularly reminiscent of Courbet; if anything, the green colours in the ships in the background and the delight in the rigging, which is also found in the prints, are close to Manet.

At this time, both painters had certain elements in common; for instance, a

---

[1] Letter of about 1863. Library of Congress, Washington.   [2] Op. cit., I. p. 88.

mutual admiration for *Japonaiserie*, for the writings of Poe, and for Spanish painting; both painted copies after the *Group of Thirteen Cavaliers* in the Louvre, then given to Velasquez but now attributed to del Mazo. Manet, however, was more attracted by Goya than was Whistler. Yet both men enjoyed the liquid, sketchy handling of paint, which Whistler used so attractively in the *Thames in Ice*. They actually met in 1861. One wonders if Manet was in any way influenced by Whistler's work, which was shown in Paris at the *Exposition Universelle* in 1867.[1] (Manet was to paint the *Port of Le Havre*, Philadelphia Museum of Fine Art, in about 1868 and Boulogne and Bordeaux harbours in 1869 and 1871.) In later years, Whistler became highly critical of Manet and, in a typical outburst, declared that 'this artist was always *l'écolier*—the student with a certain sense of things in paint, and that is all!—he never understood that art is a positive science. One step in it leading to another. He painted, you know, in *la manière noire* —the dark pictures that look very well when you come to them at Durand-Ruel's, after wandering through rooms of screaming blues and violets and greens.'[2] And he even rated Frith's *Derby Day* as the equal to a Manet!

The first years of the 1860s are a tribute to Whistler's energy; he had won a position in Paris. It was an indication of his reputation there that Fantin-Latour should have included him in his famous *Hommage à Delacroix* (Louvre) of 1864 which was a manifesto of the French *avant-garde*.[3] In London he had made his mark as a painter of the Thames as well as of figure subjects and he was known in both capitals, to the discerning few, as one of the most brilliant and radical contemporary etchers. He was in the throes of discovering his potentialities and of finding out those themes best suited to his capacities. And his correspondence with Fantin-Latour bears witness to the process of self-realisation that was then going on. There was nothing tired or pessimistic about his attitude; on the contrary, he was eager to achieve a distinctive position; his were the means and the drive to do so. He could have remained a realist painter, one who might have fulfilled the rôle of an English Manet (or, at any rate, a Carolus-Duran or a Bonvin), and perhaps he could have proceeded into Impressionism. But neither route satisfied his ambition, and the subsequent years witnessed his evolution into an artist who, whatever else may be said about him, at least worked out a style—one absolutely his own and really very different from those of his colleagues on either side of the Channel.

[1] Manet, in fact, first painted the sea in 1864; cf. Anne Coffin Hanson, 'A Group of Marine Paintings by Manet', in *The Art Bulletin*, xliv (1962), pp. 332–4.

[2] Pennell, II, p. 261.

[3] Degas was quoted by Paul Poujard as saying: 'In our beginnings Fantin, Whistler and I were all on the same road, the road from Holland. Go and see at the exhibition at the Quai Malaquais a small picture, a *scène de toilette* by Fantin; we could have signed it, Whistler and I.' *Degas Letters*, ed. Marcel Guérin, 1947, p. 236.

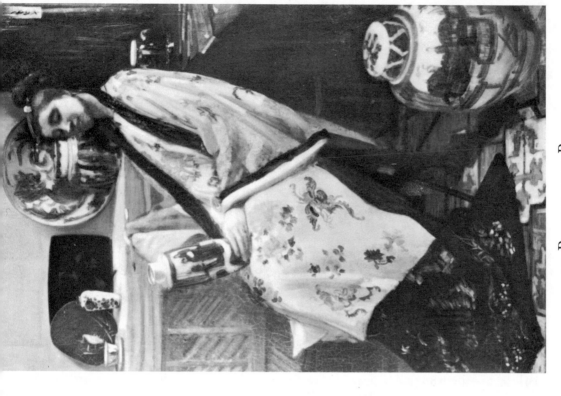

13 PURPLE AND ROSE:
THE LANGE LIJZEN OF THE SIX MARKS.
Canvas, 36 × 24 in. Signed and dated 'Whistler 1864'.
John G. Johnson Collection, Philadelphia.

12 SYMPHONY IN WHITE No. 2:
THE LITTLE WHITE GIRL.
Canvas, 30 × 20 in. Signed 'Whistler'. 1864. Exhibited
at the Royal Academy, 1865. Tate Gallery, London.

14 HARMONY IN BLUE AND SILVER: TROUVILLE.
Canvas, 19½ × 29¾ in. 1865. The figure in the foreground is Courbet. Isabella Stewart Gardner Museum, Boston, Mass.

15 CREPUSCULE IN FLESH COLOUR AND GREEN: VALPARAISO.
Canvas, 22½ × 29¾ in. Inscribed, signed and dated 'Whistler Valparaiso 66'. Tate Gallery, London.

THREE

The Road to Evasion

THE decisive impact made by Far Eastern art on European painting in the nineteenth century is a familiar chapter in the history of art.[1] Thus Whistler's own artistic conceptions and practice were radically altered when his growing passion for the Far East fructified in the 1860s.[2] In his love for the Orient he was very much an American; moreover, he lived at a period when, as a result of Commodore Perry's opening up of Japan, a number of his compatriots were drawn towards this part of the world. This was no fashionable craze without consequences, but the outcome of a deep-seated need on their part; the passion for Japan, her art and her way of life, was firmly ingrained in the minds of many Americans—not least the Bostonian Brahmins. And one is probably right in interpreting this taste as a reflection of a desire for an existence and a philosophy far removed from the pressures of the increasingly materialist society which had grown up in the United States as the aftermath of the Civil War and as a result of the fierce exploitation of the nation's wealth. Thus a desire for Nirvana haunted many a civilised conscience. It was not an ephemeral phenomenon; indeed in America the Far Eastern influence has persisted into the twentieth century, and may be seen in the architecture of Frank Lloyd Wright, and the painting of Morris Graves, Mark Tobey, Larry Bigelow and Mark Rothko. As a precursor of this trend Whistler stands out as a true-blue American.

The precise date of his first introduction to Oriental art is by no means clear; it presumably occurred while he was living in the 1850s in Paris. Almost certainly he knew Hokusai's small volume of woodcuts, the *Manga*, which in 1856 belonged to Delâtre, the printer of his etchings, and which two years later was acquired by one of his circle, the engraver Félix Bracquemond. Bracquemond swiftly showed its contents to a group which beside Whistler included Degas, Fantin-Latour, Manet, Alfred Stevens, Burty and Champfleury. All became passionately

---

[1] The literature on this topic is considerable; see especially J. A. Michener, *The Floating World*, 1954; *Japanese Prints From the Early Masters to the Modern*, 1959; Hugh Honour, *Chinoiserie. The Vision of Cathay*, 1961.

[2] Bunkio Matsuki even maintained that it was partly owing to Whistler that Hokusai and Hiroshige became better known in Japan: see *Lotus*, December, 1903, p. ii.

45

enamoured of Japanese art, examples of which were available at the shop, *La Porte Chinoise*, which M and Mme De Soye opened at 220 rue de Rivoli in 1862; and from then onwards the colours and forms of the Japanese print exerted an intoxicating influence on French painting.

Japanese art also aroused enthusiasm in England, even though it affected neither artists nor style quite so strongly as in Paris. Some examples of Japanese art had been available in England for many years before then—a woodcut book by Ihara Saikaku was brought to Europe in 1692 by Engelbert Kaempfer, the historian of Japan, and had entered the British Museum at its foundation—but only in the 1850s did a knowledge of Japanese culture start to become more general. Travellers like Kinahan Cornwallis had bought Japanese paintings (possibly prints are meant) at Commodore Perry's Port of Shimodo in 1854; the periodical *Once a Week* started to publish an account of a trip to Japan in its issue of July, 1860, which was illustrated with reproductions of prints, mainly landscapes by Hiroshige; and Sherard Osborne's *Japanese Fragments* (1861) contained reproductions of Japanese prints. Moreover in 1854 an exhibition of Japanese applied art was held in London in the gallery of the Old Water Colour Society in Pall Mall, though this does not seem to have made much impact. Japanese art was also represented at the 1862 International Exhibition at South Kensington.

Whistler himself was not the first of his generation in England to favour Japanese art; already before him William Burges and E. W. Godwin,[1] both of whom were architects, owned a number of Japanese prints. The latter's biographer states that he hung Japanese prints on the plain coloured walls of his Bristol house, 21 Portland Square; however, Ellen Terry, who met him in 1861 and became his mistress, though referring in her autobiography[2] to his Persian rugs, did not speak of Japanese prints. Presumably Whistler's close friendship with Godwin, whom he met possibly for the first time in 1863, contributed to his growing taste for *Japonaiserie*. Yet although Godwin was probably his precursor, as far as England was concerned, Whistler's rôle was undeniable: he revealed the artistic significance of the Japanese print to his English colleagues. W. M. Rossetti, who himself acquired a book of uncoloured Japanese landscapes in Paris, which he sent to Ruskin, and was the writer of an interesting paper on Japanese woodcuts,[3] confirmed this: 'it was Mr Whistler, who first called my brother's attention to Japanese art: he possessed two or three woodcut books, some coloured prints, or a screen or two'.[4] Incidentally, several prints, known to have belonged to

---

[1] See Elizabeth Aslin, 'E. W. Godwin and the Japanese Taste' in *Apollo*, lxxvi (1962), pp. 779–84, and D. Harbron, *The Conscious Stone. The Life of Edward William Godwin*, 1949.

[2] *The Story of My Life*, 1908, p. 45.

[3] This paper was originally published in *The Reader* (1863): see op. cit., pp. 363–87. He stated, however, that Japanese prints lacked 'a feeling for beauty', and 'contained nothing suggesting moral beauty'.

[4] *Some Reminiscences of William Michael Rossetti*, 1902. 2 vols. 1906. Vol. I, p. 276.

Whistler, by Kiyonaga, Utamaro, Yeishi and Kunisada, were given to the British Museum by Miss Birnie Philip; others went with her bequest to the University of Glasgow.

Whistler was not exclusively interested in Japanese pictorial art; he was also a pioneer collector of Blue and White porcelain. This ware had been collected in England, as in Holland, for several hundred years before then: in the seventeenth century Queen Mary owned some good pieces; but until Whistler's arrival it was not generally sought after in Victorian times. Yet the extent of the holdings available in this country is made explicit from the art dealer Murray Marks's correspondence[1] with Rossetti over pieces that came up for sale at Christie's. The range of Whistler's own taste in Oriental porcelain is not easy to assess; but it is reasonably clear that he went in for Chinese as well as Japanese pieces which (as is now known) date from the fourteenth century; and one is probably not far wrong in assuming that he was attracted by the aesthetic appearance of an object, caring little for its country of origin or date; and, presumably, he mostly came across later items of the seventeenth and eighteenth centuries.

In the 1860s when he started his collection, Far Eastern porcelain, screens, and prints were obtainable at Farmer and Rogers' Oriental warehouse in Regent Street, the owners of which had acquired the Japanese objects from the second great exhibition of 1862; it was at this shop that Rossetti is reputed to have bought his first pieces of Blue and White which he later sold to Whistler. He also introduced his friend to the manager, Lasenby Liberty, later Sir Arthur Liberty, who subsequently in 1875 founded his own firm, Liberty's, which for many years specialised in Oriental furnishings and fabrics. Another source for Blue and White was Murray Marks, who later became an authority on Italian Renaissance bronzes. Although the evidence is not altogether clear, he apparently handled Blue and White before 1860, importing it from Holland where it was cheaper than in England and selling a certain amount to Whistler and Rossetti; later, with the advent of a buoyant market, he bought back from the two men those pieces which came from him. Whistler's example seems to have fired Rossetti's enthusiasm; Val Prinsep even maintained[2] that Rossetti had vowed that within a week he would outstrip Whistler's collection; this, he apparently did by acquiring en bloc the group formed by the Marquis d'Azeglio, the retiring Sardinian Ambassador in London. An amusing instance of their rivalry is recounted by Rossetti in a letter to his mother from Paris in 1864, which described how he had purchased four Japanese books from Madame De Soye and that 'all the costumes were being snapped up by a French artist, Tissot, who, it seems, is doing three Japanese pictures, which the mistress of the shop described to me as the three

---

[1] G. C. Williamson, *Murray Marks and his Friends*, 1919, passim.
[2] Cited by Oswald Doughty in *A Victorian Romantic: Dante Gabriel Rossetti*, 1949, pp. 313–14.

wonders of the world, evidently in her opinion quite throwing Whistler into the shade. She told me, with a great deal of laughing about Whistler's consternation at my collection of China.'[1]

It was hardly surprising, in view of his craze for Oriental art, that Whistler came to be known as the 'Japanese artist'; and Mr James Laver reminds us that 'it was under that name that he was pointed out to Walter Greaves as he sat painting in the window of his first Chelsea house'.[2] As soon as he settled in, Whistler, who always liked to make a decorative setting for himself, started to decorate his home with Oriental art, and, in her charming way, his mother reported that 'this artistic abode of my son is ornamented by a very rare collection of Japanese and Chinese. He considers the paintings upon them the finest specimens of art, and his companions (artists), who resort here for an evening's relaxation occasionally, get enthusiastic as they handle and examine the curious figures portrayed. . . . He has also a Japanese book of paintings, unique in their estimation. You will not wonder that Jemie's inspiration should be (under such influences) of the same cast.'[3]

Nevertheless, unlike some of his French contemporaries—Manet, for instance —Whistler was not exclusively taken by the Japanese print with its bold colours and striking forms, or by Blue and White; he was fascinated by the Far Eastern spirit in general. Appropriately, early in 1865, Fantin-Latour introduced him clad in a kimono into his now destroyed picture *Le Toast*.[4] In the first instance, Whistler's use of Oriental elements in his own pictures was touched with a similar fancy-dress spirit. In his earliest Oriental subject picture, *Rose and Silver: La Princesse du Pays de la Porcelaine* (seen in Fig. 35), in the Freer Gallery, Washington, which is the portrait, finished after innumerable sittings, of Christine Spartali, the daughter of the Greek Consul-General in London and a friend of the Ionides family, she not only wears a kimono, albeit a trifle self-consciously, but her pose is derived from that of a Japanese print. In spite of its Japanese character, the general impression made by the completed canvas is dissimilar from the radical design found in Japanese prints. However, the *Japonaiserie* element in this composition is more marked in the freely painted preliminary oil sketch in the Worcester Art Museum, Mass. The finished picture or the *Purple and Rose: The Lange Lijzen of the Six Marks* (Fig. 13), painted in 1864 and now in the John G. Johnson collection, Philadelphia, in which the objects shown, as

¹ Letter of 12th November, 1864. See *D. G. Rossetti: His Family Letters*. With a memoir by W. M. Rossetti, 2 vols., 1895. Vol. II, p. 180.

² Op. cit., p. 97.

³ Letter of 2nd October, 1864. 'The Lady of the Portrait'. Op. cit., pp. 318–28.

⁴ Cf. L. Bénédite, 'Histoire d'un Tableau, "Le Toast" par Fantin-Latour', in *Revue de l'Art Ancien et Moderne*, xvii (1905), pp. 21–31, 121–36. The head and shoulders of Whistler, cut out from the canvas, is now in the Freer Gallery, Washington.

II. CAPRICE IN PURPLE AND GOLD, No. 2: THE GOLDEN SCREEN. Wood panel (19¾ x 27 in.). Signed and dated, Whistler 1864. This is one of the artist's most successful pictures in the Japanese taste (The Freer Gallery of Art, Washington).

well as the carpet, belonged to the artist, betray a certain Victorian frowstiness; as if we were being shown some old Curio Shop.

The disposition of the space, in fact, in these two pictures, which are among the most overtly Japanese of his paintings, is by no means Oriental. Only with the *Caprice in Purple: The Golden Screen* (Plate II) of 1864 (Freer Gallery, Washington), did Whistler start to simplify the construction and impose a rhythmical pattern on it, thus giving decorative unity to the picture. But in spite of Jo's Japanese costume and the Hiroshige prints which are on the floor and decorate the screen, the scene is conceived as something of a masquerade. Even when the lay-out of a picture seems to derive from a Japanese print—as is the case with the *Variations in Flesh Colour and Gold: The Balcony* in the Freer Gallery, Washington, which is connected with Kiyonaga's *Three Girls at a Window* (forming one of the *Twelve Scenes in Shinawaga*)—Whistler combined the scene with a background composed of the Thames with an outline of factories; however deep his taste for the exotic he did not propose to forget the local scene. His derivation from this particular Japanese master is significant and E. F. Strange once pointed out[1] that Whistler's own collection included works by this artist who favoured lighter, more delicate colours, and not the later men who went in for strong and often garish aniline ones. Nevertheless, the colours in this picture—as in others from the same period—are relatively powerful; the recumbent girl wears an orange dress and mauves, reds, greens, yellows and blues are boldly used.

Whistler's love of Japanese art is central to any understanding of his personality and his art. Of course, there is an element of truth in Sickert's sharp contention that with this passion, 'Whistler, instead of the cobra who had swallowed the goat, was rather like a cobra who wondered whether he hadn't better become a goat'.[2] Nevertheless, his art was fundamentally influenced by that of the Far East; and his basic conception of harmony was an Oriental one. Many years later he told the Pennells[3] that, for him, the Japanese influence meant the maintenance of a tradition, and not a revolution, in European art; art, he claimed, was unchangeable, and his own work had been the same at the beginning as at the end. Moreover, when Mortimer Menpes explained to him the principles of Japanese draughtsmanship (the Kyôsai method), he considered them to be identical with his own.[4] In this connection, his considerable experiments as an etcher may have been partly influenced by the Japanese ideals; for, at this time, the etching, as a sort of *art libre*, served as an important weapon in the struggle against the automatic routine associated with academic art.[5] Nevertheless, somewhat para-

---

[1] *The Colour Prints of Hiroshige* (no date), pp. 125–6.
[2] *A Free House!* ed. by Osbert Sitwell, 1947, p. 26.
[3] *Journal*, p. 31.   [4] *Whistler as I Knew Him*, 1904, p. 41.
[5] Cf. Ernst Scheyer, 'Far Eastern Art and French Impressionism', in the *Art Quarterly*, vi (1943), pp. 117–42.

doxically, those works in which the subject matter is not ostensibly Oriental—
the prints and Nocturnes—provide the most effective illustration in his art of the
qualities associated with Far Eastern art.

For Whistler, the 1860s were essentially *wanderjähre*: this was the era when
he was searching around for the formulae which would best suit him and answer
to his aspirations. Of some significance was his visit to Amsterdam in 1863; there
he was able to pick up cheaply some attractive pieces of Blue and White and
deepen his appreciation of seventeenth-century Dutch painting. Dutch pictures
would certainly have come his way in Paris and London, but to see a national
school in its local context is invariably rewarding; and one may assume that this
short trip fostered his love of Terborch and Hals, two of his favourite artists.
Unfortunately, his letters from Holland to Fantin-Latour do not provide any
details about his experiences; how tantalising to read in one of them no more
than *The Night Watch* is something quite different from what he thought it
was.[1]

And what of Vermeer? Is it possible that on this visit he began to appreciate
Vermeer, and is it entirely fanciful to detect an echo of this master's spirit in the
Purple and Rose: The Lange Lijzen of the Six Marks (Fig. 13), which was painted
a year later? Some reminiscence of Dutch art would have been appropriate in
this picture in view of its theme; thus it is just worth emphasising that, at around
this date, Vermeer's name was becoming known in advanced French circles owing
to the advocacy of the perceptive critic Thoré-Bürger.[2] Moreover, Whistler had
the chance of seeing this painter's works in London, as no fewer than two of his
most important pictures, *The Concert* (Isabella Stewart Gardner Museum, Boston)
and *The Astronomer* (Private collection, Paris), passed through Christie's rooms
in 1860 and 1864 respectively, both years in which the painter was in that city.
As artists often frequented auctions at this time, it is just conceivable that, though
presumably unaware of their identity, he may have come across them; for so
quick-witted and responsive a person as Whistler this would have sufficed.
Something of Vermeer's spirit could have touched his own; and, significantly,
grey is a predominant tonality in the Boston picture. Moreover, his collection of
photographs contained a reproduction of Vermeer's *Little Street* in the Mauritshuis,
The Hague. In painting the *Lange Lijzen*, Whistler may also have remembered
Corot's figure pieces of the 1860s; these also possess an affinity with the Delft
master, and a decided connection with Corot is apparent in several of his later works.

Some insight into Whistler's mind during the 1860s may be gained from his
letters to Fantin-Latour, in one of which he complained that 'I am horribly
depressed at the moment. It's always the same—work that's so hard and uncertain.

---

[1] Undated letter of 1863 from the Hotel Brack, Doelen, Amsterdam. Library of Congress, Washington.

[2] See his *Les Musées de Hollande*, 1858: his study on Vermeer appeared in the *Gazette des Beaux-Arts*
in 1866.

I am *so slow*. When will I achieve a more rapid way of painting—when I say that,
I mean to say something different; you will understand what I'm driving at. I
produce so little, because I rub out so much. Oh! Fantin, I know so little. Things
don't go so quickly.'[1] And he confessed that two small pictures of the Thames
which he had just finished did not give him much pleasure. The upshot of this
self-criticism was clear enough; he was discouraged by his technical shortcomings.
Nevertheless, his objective of a rapid and fluid manner of painting was admirably demonstrated in his sketches for pictures like *Rose and Silver: La Princesse
du Pays de la Porcelaine* and *Variations in Flesh Colour and Gold: the Balcony*,
which are in the Worcester Art Museum, Mass., and in the Birnie Philip Bequest,
Glasgow, respectively. These pictures indicate the way in which the palette knife
was used to provide sharp accents—broad sweeps of paint give just the rapid
note he sought; the latter sketch also shows how he favoured a wide range of
colours—orange, pink, blue, mauve, red, grey, green and pale white. However,
as he admitted, it was one thing to dash off a sketch, quite another to carry through
a major composition.

The mid-1860s formed a particularly decisive moment in Whistler's career.
He was in the midst of discovering a new and fresh way of handling paint; this
freer and more evocative style appeared when, after a trip to Cologne, he and Jo
settled at Trouville in August-September, 1865, where Courbet, Monet and
Daubigny were then established. These were happy days. Years later, Courbet
in a letter[2] to Whistler recalled how at that time Jo would act the clown to amuse
them, in the evening singing Irish songs, with spirit and distinction. Courbet
spoke of a midnight flit from the casino of the hotel to the sea where they bathed
on the icy beach. They would enjoy shrimp salads with fresh butter; they ate
cutlets for lunch which stoked them up for painting the sea. Courbet's letter
reveals that 'space' and 'the horizon' preoccupied them. The emphasis upon space
is significant; many of the pictures Whistler painted there—*The Crepuscule in Opal*
(Toledo Museum of Art); *Grey and Green: The Silver Sea* (The Art Institute,
Chicago); the *Blue and Silver: Trouville* (Freer Gallery, Washington); and the
Harmony in Blue and Silver: Trouville (Gardner Museum, Boston)—are distinguished by their suggestion of space, an enchanted vision too. The touches of
impasto found in the Toledo and Freer pictures and the arrangement of the
compositions point to his dependence on Courbet, then, so this artist told his friend
and patron Bruyas, painting autumn skies, 'each more extraordinary and freer than
the other'.[3] Courbet definitely considered Whistler as his pupil, and presumably
he was referring to the younger man's pictures of this period when he said he

[1] Undated letter from London, 1863–64. Library of Congress, Washington.
[2] See letter from Vaud of 14th February, 1877, in University of Glasgow. This will be published by
Mr McLaren Young.
[3] Letter of January, 1866. Cited by G. Riat, *Gustave Courbet*, 1906, p. 229.

had talent, *le petit Whistler*, but he would always paint the sky too low, or the horizon too high.[1]

It was at Trouville that Courbet painted the magnificent portrait of Jo—*The Woman in the Mirror*, of which four versions are known,[2] while Whistler portrayed Courbet in the *Harmony in Blue and Silver: Trouville* (Fig. 14: Gardner Museum, Boston). This lovely canvas is possibly conceived as a delicate compliment to his master since it could be a recollection of the *Seashore at Palavas* of 1854 in the Musée Fabre, Montpellier; in it Whistler started to treat the composition on one plane, touching in the colours with light sketchy strokes. This same sort of technique he used freely and poetically in the many small seascapes which date from the 1880s onwards.

The sea held a special, exciting quality for Whistler and played a large part in his affections; his love for the sea which is so noticeable during his life is one of his most sympathetic characteristics. This fondness for the deserted seashore was typical of the Romantics, from Shelley onwards, and his lines from *Julian and Maddalo* express the attitude which we may sense in Whistler's pictures.

> *. . . I love all waste*
> *And solitary places; where we taste*
> *The pleasure of believing what we see*
> *Is boundless, as we wish our souls to be.*

This was a note sounded by Rossetti and Swinburne, both friends of Whistler's, and by Matthew Arnold in various poems. His love for the sea was strengthened when from February to November, 1866, he paid his mysterious visit to South America. The reasons which prompted this expedition are obscure; his own account is inconclusive. Did it arise from a Conradian desire for adventure, a need to escape from domestic problems, or from a wish to see the Pacific with its Oriental character? All are possible. Most of his time in South America was spent in Chile, and in Valparaiso, where he seems to have been during one of the many revolutions. He painted in Valparaiso—or, at any rate, worked out there the ideas for—about half-a-dozen seascapes, which are more individual than the Trouville series.

One of the chief differences between a picture like *Crepuscule in Flesh Colour and Green: Valparaiso* (Fig. 15), in the Tate Gallery, London—possibly the most exquisite of the group—and the earlier, Trouville paintings is that the tones composing the surface of the canvas are blended more skilfully than before; the ships are not so much imposed upon the picture as worked into the general

---

[1] Letter to his father of 17th November, 1865. Cited by Riat, op. cit., p. 228. See also *A Free House!* p. 15.

[2] The best known is in the Metropolitan Museum, New York: two other versions are in the National Museum, Stockholm, and the Kansas City Art Gallery.

16 Symphony in Grey and Green: The Ocean.
Canvas, 31 × 38⅞ in. About 1866–67. Frick Collection, New York.

17 SYMPHONY IN WHITE No. 3.

Canvas, 20¼ × 30⅞ in. Inscribed, signed and dated
'Symphony in White No. III. Whistler, 1867'.
Barber Institute of Fine Arts, Birmingham.

18 THE WHITE GIRL No. 4.

Canvas, 76½ × 39¼ in. Butterfly signature.
First exhibited 1874. Fogg Art Museum,
Cambridge, Mass.

composition and in such a way as to avoid disturbing the tonalities. Although the streaky sky acknowledges the debt to Courbet, the move towards a more unified surface treatment is evident; and the aesthetic quality of his vision starts to predominate. Thus in the *Morning after the Revolution, Valparaiso* (Birnie Philip Bequest, Glasgow), no political comment (we presume) is intended. In such pictures he was after, as Professor Pevsner once remarked,[1] 'an impression, quickly passing effects of light and atmosphere—the attitude in short which we attribute to the Impressionist painter', and, as he continued, 'as examples of Impressionism, such pictures are surprisingly precocious'. Yet why did Whistler refrain from continuing in this vein, and going on to become an Impressionist proper? The differences reside in the intention; the Impressionist was eager to analyse Nature, more or less scientifically, but, for his part, Whistler sought a selective vision of Nature, one suitable for the creation of his own arrangement. In one of his most lyrical pictures, *Symphony in Grey and Green: The Ocean* (Fig. 16), in the Frick Collection, New York, certainly painted prior to 1867, the effects are heightened and brought out by the appearance in the foreground of a few distinctly Oriental-looking branches and the use of a signature, written as if in Chinese or Japanese characters.

This is an extremely beautiful painting in which the greyish tonality of the water is relieved by the use of purplish tints, while the ships and the jetty are rendered by means of swift strokes. Its essence lies in the tasteful manipulation of tonalities; and the overall decorative effect is further heightened by the frame with its butterfly motifs. A similar decorative quality is apparent in the *Nocturne, Blue and Gold, Valparaiso*, in the Freer Gallery, Washington, where, apparently for the first time, he painted a proper night scene—one which must be considered as the prelude to the London Nocturnes. He also used dabs of paint in this canvas in order to indicate the presence and position of gaslights, a technique more fully exploited in *Nocturne in Black and Gold: The Falling Rocket* (Plate IV) of 1875, in the Detroit Institute of Arts; at the same time, no attempt was made to provide a recessional perspective; the surface is composed almost on one plane, as in a Japanese print. There can be little doubt that contact with the Pacific occasioned a deepening of Whistler's sensibility; this helped to prepare the way for the Nocturnes.

During the mid-1860s, while retaining certain realist affiliations, Whistler was deeply and increasingly attracted by the ideal trend of the time; in fact he was to turn his back on much that up till then he had cherished. In this connection his friendship with Albert Moore is important. Although today this minor classicist painter is largely forgotten, his pictures appealed to several of the English *avant garde*, including Swinburne, who maintained that 'his painting is

[1] 'Whistler's "Valparaiso Harbour" at the Tate Gallery,' *Burlington Magazine*, lxxix (1941), pp. 115 ff.

to the artists what the verse of Théophile Gautier is to the poets: the faultless
and secure expression of an exclusive worship of things beautiful'.[1] Whistler had
actually met Moore in 1865, the year before going to Chile, and must have seen
The Marble Seat (once in the Philip H. Rathbone collection) at the Royal Academy.
He was one of the few contemporary artists for whom he was prepared to spare
a good word. 'Albert Moore', he declared in a typical sally. 'Poor fellow! The
greatest artist that, in the century, England might have cared for and called her
own—how sad for him to live there—how mad to die in that land of important
ignorance and Beadledom.'[2]

The flowing draperies, languorous females and decorative appeal of Moore's
pictures had clearly much to offer Whistler, who was increasingly preoccupied
with decorative painting. Pictures like the *Four Seasons*, which had been shown
at the Royal Academy in 1864, and *Pomegranates*, on view there two years later,
are clearly related to the sort of work he was doing at this time and continued to
do during the late 1860s; for instance, Moore's *Pomegranates* depicts three girls
in white robes partly covered with semi-transparent shades of red, while the central
figure is kneeling before a cabinet; this is not far removed from the type of composition found in the *Symphony in White No. 3* (Fig. 17) in the Barber Institute
of Fine Art, Birmingham, and the *Symphony in White No. 4* (Fig. 20), of which one
version is in the Tate Gallery, London.

It is always difficult to determine precisely how much in an artist's contribution
is due to direct influence and how much arises from the contemporary intellectual
climate; in the case of Whistler and Moore (whom Whistler wished to co-opt
as a member of the *Société des Trois* after he had fallen out with Legros in 1867)
both men were clearly closely interested in similar themes and with the evocation
of the same sort of mood.

Not surprisingly, a contretemps arose a few years later, at some date around
September, 1870, when Whistler felt that confusion might be occasioned by the
apparent resemblance between his own and Moore's style. In what, for him, was
a generous and tactful letter,[3] he pointed out that he had shown two of his friend's
'beautiful sketches to Leyland' and, 'while admiring them as you know I must
do everything of yours—more than the production of any living man—it struck
me dimly—perhaps that one of my own sketches of girls in the seashore was in
motive not unlike your yellow one—of course I don't mean in scheme of colour
but in general sentiment of movement and in the place of the sea, sky and shore,
etc.'. In order to clear up this position he suggested that Moore and Billy Nesfield
should visit his studio and examine the picture in question, 'the one in blue green

---

[1] 'Notes on some Pictures of 1868 (at the Royal Academy)', in *Essays and Studies*, 1897, p. 360.
[2] Cited by A. L. Baldry, *Albert Moore*, 1904, p. 25. Whistler dedicated *Whistler v. Ruskin: Art and Art Critics* (1878) to Moore.
[3] Letter of about September, 1870, in the University of Glasgow.

and flesh colour of four girls careering along the seashore, one with a parasol', and give their findings. He could not have suggested a better arbitrator than Nesfield, 'a fat, jolly hearted fellow, genuinely good natured, very fond of smoking, and I deeply grieve to say of women',[1] who was also a collector with eclectic tastes and a partner of Richard Norman Shaw, the architect.

On 19th September, Nesfield pronounced: 'Thus I strongly feel that you have seen and felt Moore's specialité in his female figures' method of clothing and use of coloured muslin; also his hard study of Greek work. Then Moore has thoroughly appreciated and felt your mastery of painting in a light key.' But, he went on, 'there is no harm in both painting in a similar way as the effect and treatment are so wide apart'.[2] It was a just summary of a delicate matter, and one in which the connections—and the differences—between the work of the two men were properly assessed.

One picture especially close in spirit to Moore's work is the *Symphony in White No. 3* (Fig. 17), which represents Jo and Milly Jones, the wife of an actor called Robson. He was engaged on this in 1866 and it was shown at the Royal Academy in the following year—the first of his works to bear a musical title. In adopting a musical terminology for the nomenclature of many of his works—and a number were subsequently retitled to accord with this principle—Whistler was especially anxious to emphasis that the artist's business lay, not with story-telling, but with the science and art of picture-making. His purpose was to provide a suggested way of looking at his works; this accorded with the general conception of the colouristic effects sought; in other words, the various shades of colour employed required to be related harmoniously one to the other and in reference to a central principle. By this, however, he did not propose an automatic restriction of his colour range to one colour alone, and in his effective dismissal of P. G. Hamerton, who had quite failed to appreciate his aims, he pointed out: '*Bon Dieu!* did this wise person expect white hair and chalked faces? And does he then, in his astounding ignorance, believe that a symphony in F contains no other note, but shall be a continual repetition of F. F. F. . . . . Fool!'[3]

Whistler himself, though not particularly musical, was sufficiently quick to realise that certain sides of a sister art could offer an aesthetic principle which accorded with, and suited, his aims. He may have picked up the idea of employing musical titles from Paul Mantz, who had used the phrase *symphonie du blanc* in 1863 to describe the *White Girl*.[4] But he was also surely sufficiently involved with French aesthetic artistic circles to have remembered that one of the characters in Murger's novel had composed a *Symphonie sur l'influence du bleu dans les arts*;

---

[1] Simeon Solomon to A. C. Swinburne (late September, 1869), *The Swinburne Letters*, Vol. I, p. 32.

[2] Letter of 19th September, 1870, in the University of Glasgow.

[3] Chelsea, June, 1867, *The Gentle Art of Making Enemies*, p. 45.

[4] Pennell, I, p. 103. This was before the artist himself had begun to employ musical titles.

that Gautier had written a poem entitled *Symphonie en blanc majeur*; and that this writer had ventilated analogous ideas in his other writings. Theories concerning the relationship between music and painting were current at this time; also the view that music was the highest form of artistic expression, and his compatriot Poe, whose influence on French writing was considerable, had claimed in his *Essay on the Poetic Principle* that 'in music perhaps the soul most nearly attains the great end for which, when inspired by the Poetic Sentiment, it struggles—the creation of supernal Beauty'. Likewise Whistler had possibly read or, at any rate, heard about Baudelaire's articles on the *Exposition Universelle* and the Salon of 1859, in which this writer had discussed the rôle of the imagination, hinting at that correspondence between the arts which he subsequently examined in greater detail. Moreover, Whistler may well have found some support for his use of musical terms in discussions with Fantin-Latour, to whom music afforded a profound inspiration and whose *Hommage à Tannhäuser* was exhibited in the Salon of 1864; nevertheless, both men saw the connection between music and painting in very different terms.

Yet, finally, there is not much to be said about the relationship between Whistler's art and music; the main point is that the analogy between painting and music above all enabled him to provide an easily grasped definition of his aims. In any case, the connection between music and painting is tenuous at best: the differences are far more striking than the resemblances, and, naturally, if these did not obtain, there would be no real reason for their separate existence.

Nevertheless, Whistler's apprehension of the importance of music for the painter enabled him to understand that the building up of pictorial tones does relate to the principles of musical composition. The art of painting, as he saw it, consisted of just this: the blending into a harmony of the disparate colours available to the painter, either in Nature or on the palette. The importance of this phase is that in the same year as the *Symphony in White No. 3* was hung at the Academy, Whistler revealed that he was groping towards a conception of art running counter to his original realist beliefs. This conception was allied to the contemporary ideal trend; that his attempts to give body to these new ideas occasioned difficulty he admitted in an important letter to his usual confidant Fantin-Latour.[1] 'Courbet and his influence was disgusting. The regret, rage and even the hate that I now feel for all that will perhaps astonish you, but here's the explanation. It is not poor Courbet nor his works which repulse me. As always, I recognise the qualities of the man and his art. I am not even complaining of the influence his painting had on my own. He did not have any and it can't be found in my canvases. There could not be any, in fact, because mine is a very personal approach and I am rich in qualities which he doesn't have, and which suffice me. 'This is the reason why all that he represented was bad for me. It is because

[1] In a letter of 1867 (August) from Lindsey Row, Chelsea. Library of Congress, Washington.

this damned Realism made an immediate appeal to my vanity as a painter, and mocking all that tradition stands for, cried aloud with the assurance of ignorance: "Long live Nature." Nature—that cry, *mon cher*, was the greatest misfortune for me. Where could one find an apostle readier to accept this theory so known for itself, so calming for worries. What! He had only to open his eyes and paint what he saw in front of him—beautiful Nature and all that stuff. It was not only that. Very well, you will see. Thus one saw the *Piano*, *La Fille Blanche*, the *Thames*, the seascapes . . . canvases, in fact, produced by a scamp who was swollen with the vanity of trying to show to his friends splendid gifts, qualities which only demand a severe education to make their possessor a master the moment that he is one, and not a debauched scholar . . . Ah! *mon ami*, our little group has been a society of . . . Ah! if only I had been a pupil of Ingres. I don't say that out of any rhapsodical enthusiasm for his pictures; I like them half-heartedly. I found many of the pictures, which we saw together, of a very questionable style, not at all Greek, as is maintained, but very viciously French. I feel that one has much further to go and much more beautiful things to paint. But I repeat—if only I had been his pupil; what a master he would have proved, and how he would have healthily led us.'

In the course of this long communication he also ventilated his views on the relationship between drawing and colour—'when properly guided by her master, drawing, colour is a splendid girl'; as a whole his statement is indicative of the alteration then occurring in his ideas and consequently in his art. Yet his admiration for Ingres did not mean that his work, in any real sense, came close to that of this master; he clearly treated him with reserve.

Although too much ought not to be made of his interest in Baudelaire (whom, of course, he knew) and in French aesthetic theory, it may be recalled that in enunciating his conception of the 'Heroism of Modern Life' in the Salon of 1845, the poet had maintained that Ingres and Courbet had sacrificed the imaginative faculty on the altars of other gods—those of 'the great tradition' and 'external nature' respectively. Baudelaire's attitude was not all that dissimilar from Whistler's; he admired both artists but neither satisfied him.

These were testing years for Whistler. He had by no means found his way and had even perhaps embarked on the wrong direction as far as his talents were concerned. Yet many of his pictures of the late 1860s show his eagerness to employ an ideal style—after his own fashion. This induced him, rather unsuccessfully as it turned out, to try and embody his researches into a series of large-scale canvases of figure subjects; for instance, Whistler intended to paint a big picture in which the artist himself, his models, Fantin-Latour and Moore, were to be depicted in his studio; he may well have been led to take up this idea, as Mr McLaren Young has suggested,[1] by the example of Fantin-Latour's

[1] *Whistler Catalogue*, p. 45.

Le Toast (1864) or Courbet's *L'Atelier* (1855). His painting, so he informed Fantin-Latour,[1] would express everything that would shock the Academicians; although the final picture was never executed, its appearance may be assessed from the two oil sketches in the Art Institute, Chicago (Fig. 19) and the Municipal Gallery of Modern Art, Dublin; these suffice to give some idea of its charm and elegance.

It was in line with this programme that, in about 1867, he considered painting a life-size version of *Variations in Flesh Colour and Gold: The Balcony*, a project which engaged him for a number of years; the oil sketch, in the Birnie Philip Bequest at Glasgow, may have been only one part of this plan. It was significant, too, of his preoccupations at this period that he should have started a painting on the theme of one of Poe's poems—'Annabel Lee'. This was seen in its early stages by William Graham, the M.P. and well-known patron of the Pre-Raphaelites and collector of early Italian art, who paid for it but never secured its delivery; the picture failed to satisfy Whistler and it now exists in a rubbed down condition at Glasgow. Nevertheless, he took immense pains to establish the composition and various versions of the theme survive, among them a sketch in the Birnie Philip Bequest, Glasgow, and a delightful pastel in the Freer Gallery, Washington. Moreover, the existence of a number of chalk drawings of girls represented in the same pose suggests that he had tried out the idea in this medium before embarking on the picture itself, in the event to prove abortive. These drawings are typical of the sketches of fragile and elegant girls which date from this period; this was an approach used frequently in subsequent years.

Whistler's attempt at this time to create a new and ideal style evidently encountered difficulties. He was tempted to paint another 'Symphony in White' —this was to be No. 4 and this project engaged him during the winter of 1868–9; but the various pencil and ink drawings, as well as pastels, relating to this composition, reveal the trials he underwent in trying to formulate the picture. Nevertheless, a drawing at Glasgow, which presents the figures in the poses adopted in one of the oil versions, seems to suggest that he had actually worked out the idea at a relatively early stage. The relationship between the various studies and versions is difficult to disentangle; but what would appear to be the oil sketch for the picture is now in the Freer Gallery, Washington; a later, more elaborate, version, with some variants, is in the Tate Gallery (Fig. 20). A comparison between the oil sketch and the Tate Gallery's picture is instructive, indicating that the freedom and spontaneity of the earlier venture—the sketch—had been subdued, and to the disadvantage of the later work; but this was perhaps inevitable in view of the artist's ambition to relate all the elements in the picture by means of uniform tonalities.

There would seem to be little doubt that, in its sketch form, this composition,

[1] Letter of 16th August, 1866. Library of Congress, Washington.

as well as a group of five other and similar sketches, were originally conceived to form part of a decorative ensemble; the four horizontal pictures of women are all roughly of identical size and are executed in the same technique; in fact, the Pennells connected them with an entry in W. M. Rossetti's diary for July 28th, 1867, which stated that 'Whistler is doing on a largish scale for Leyland the subject of women with flowers, and has made coloured sketches of four or five other subjects of the like class, very promising in point of conception and of

THE DESK
Etching, $8\frac{3}{8} \times 5\frac{3}{8}$ in. Messrs P. and D. Colnaghi, London.

colour and arrangement'.[1] The *Six Projects*, in the Freer Gallery, Washington, hold a special place in Whistler's development owing to their subject matter and technique; they may be connected with oil sketches like the study for *Rose and Silver: La Princesse du Pays de la Porcelaine*, which is probably slightly earlier in date, though the handling has become freer, more daring and instinctive; the figures are rendered with calligraphic simplicity and much is staked on the liquidity of the paint itself. Whistler stands out as a bold, even succulent, colourist: thus in the *Symphony in Blue and Pink* (Fig. 22), the white and green garments are con-

[1] Pennell, I, p. 149. This comes from *Rossetti Papers, 1862 to 1870*, by W. M. Rossetti, 1903, p. 320.

trasted with the blue pink-streaked sky, while in the *Variations in White and Red*, a mauve sky supports a blue sea in which yellows, browns and dashes of pink are also discernible. The novelty of his colouring at this point almost anticipates the boldness of Fauvism. In this group of oils, as in the related pastels and drawings, he revealed his skill in suggesting the tender sensuality of half-clad female figures—these are girls who have not yet achieved their maturity and whose appeal partly lies in their innocence and in our awareness of their potentialities. Their slender forms, half-orientalised, half-hellenised, are in some ways akin to those found in certain Pre-Raphaelite pictures or in Puvis de Chavannes; they may be related, though at some remove, to the maidens in Botticelli's *Primavera*; and what of Proust's *Jeunes filles en fleurs*?

Two very unexpected figures of Venus, also in the Freer Gallery, Washington, are presumably connected with this series, although not apparently designed with a specific decorative purpose in mind. (He made an etching of Venus at this time.) In the *Venus Rising from the Sea* (Fig. 21), Whistler took a theme with obvious classical connections which had also been treated by his hero of the moment, Ingres, in the picture of *Venus Anadyomene*, 1848, at Chantilly. As a colour study Whistler's picture is most delicate; an outline of brown paint encloses the body, the leaves are pink and rose-coloured, while a purple streak tinges the far-distance. Nevertheless, Whistler could hardly sustain a challenge of this sort, and this picture underlines the difficulties facing him when trying to paint the nude; it is wistful and delicate and, characteristically, pink and red blossoms are introduced into the foreground; however its tentative and rather half-hearted appearance almost seems to suggest that the theme itself frightened him; perhaps a sort of innate puritanism made him reluctant to come to grips with the nude.

On the whole, this group of pictures is usually overlooked in the study of the artist; it is a type of painting not usually associated with his style and certainly unpopular today, but these works are of major importance for an understanding of his point of view and for his subsequent evolution. It is significant that, towards the end of his life, he should have reverted to painting pictures of this type. Yet in the 1860s he abandoned them, and one may reasonably argue that his attempt at a novel and 'ideal' style failed. One reason for this was surely his inability to surmount the technical difficulties entailed by large-scale figure-painting of the sort he had in mind; a wider range of colour was required than was at his disposal; and, in any case, perhaps this way of painting did not really suit him.

The character of the subject matter in this group is especially fascinating. It shows his desire to combine his liking for *Japonaiserie* with a new found love of late Greek art, doubtless prompted by his friendship with Albert Moore. The neo-classical strain in Victorian painting is an extremely interesting phenomenon —one that requires detailed study in its own right; it affected a number of artists, among them Alma-Tadema, who started to paint his famous pictures of Roman

19 THE ARTIST'S STUDIO.

Panel, 24¾ × 18¾ in. About 1867–68. One of two sketches for a large picture that was never painted. Art Institute, Chicago.

20 THREE FIGURES
PINK AND GREY.

Canvas, 55½ × 72 in.
About 1868. Tate
Gallery, London.

21 VENUS RISING
FROM THE SEA.

Canvas, 23½ × 19¼ i
About 1868. Freer
Gallery of Art,
Washington.

life in 1865,[1] and Lord Leighton, whose *Orpheus and Eurydice* dates from 1864. (Leighton's elegant chalk drawings, incidentally, often resemble Whistler's.) As far as ancient art was concerned, Whistler himself was above all attracted by Hellenistic terracottas. He was able to see originals in the house of his friend Alexander Ionides, who had purchased a considerable collection in Smyrna; those in the Louvre and the British Museum, which included the Duc de Blacas' collection, were also available to him. Moreover, during the 1870s, actual Tanagra figures, from the town of Tanagra where excavations had recently taken place, were coming onto the market.[2] Whistler evidently knew these, as a chalk drawing at Glasgow carries the title 'Tanagra'; in addition, he owned an album with more than thirty photographs of Greek terracottas and vases. Naturally, the elegant poses of the terracottas, with their flowing garments, captured his attention and clearly influenced the formation of his style; for example, the movement of the hips in a Tanagra figure like the *Aphrodite Nursing Eros* (once in the Ionides collection)[3] provides a parallel with the pastels and drawings possessing similar poses. How typical of his flair for novelty—an exhibition of Greek terra-cottas was held in Paris in 1878—and of his life-long passion for the exquisite, that such objects should have delighted him!

The reaction against realism, as embodied in his letter of 1867 to Fantin-Latour and exemplified in his work, was instrumental in leading Whistler to adopt a classicistic style. This made him take a standpoint which seems to be at variance with that usually attributed to him—as the painter of modern life. But, in this connection, one has to remember that the sense of alertness to the contemporary scene—as represented by the early pictures, and, to some extent, by the later Nocturnes—was complemented, in his make-up, by a fervent belief in the primacy of art. After all, he was essentially an aesthete and the wave of classical-ideal painting which occurred in England and on the Continent in the nineteenth century (with Ingres, Puvis de Chavannes, Leighton and Hans von Marées as its major exponents) was an affirmation of faith in the absolute necessity for, and integrity of, art—and in the chosen rôle of the artist.

The fact that Whistler had passed his impressionable student days in Paris is always relevant for the development and assessment of his ideas. During his time there one can hardly doubt that he had come across Gautier's celebrated preface to *Mademoiselle de Maupin* (1835),[4] which struck the first main blow for the concept of 'art for art's sake', one which fired the imagination of more than one generation! Gautier's theories about artistic activity as a form of play,

---

[1] Cf. Mario Amaya, 'The Roman World of Alma-Tadema' in *Apollo*, lxxvi (1962), pp. 771–778.

[2] Cf. R. A. Higgins, 'The Discovery of Tanagra Statuettes' in *Apollo*, lxxvi (1962), pp. 587–93.

[3] Repr. M. B. Huish, *Greek Terracotta Statuettes*, 1900, Fig. I.

[4] Cf. *La Préface de Mademoiselle de Maupin*, ed. G. Matoré, 1946. On Franco-British artistic and literary relations at this period, see Enid Starkie, *From Gautier to Eliot*, 1960.

about exoticism, about art as a luxury and on the insufficiency of Nature, were all ones which Whistler, more or less, endorsed. Indeed, in the very decade which witnessed Whistler's *Six Projects* and his delight in classicism, Gautier had declared: 'The aim of art is not the exact reproduction of nature, but the creation, by means of the forms and colours it offers us, of a microcosm where may exist the dreams, sensations and ideas that are inspired by the view of the external world.'[1] Under this dispensation, which foreshadowed the precepts of the Symbolists, the antique world played a major part; it represented that phase in human existence when life was passed in an atmosphere of serene beauty. In the sonnet Gautier addressed to Ingres, thanking him for the gift of a study for the *Apothéose d'Homère*, the poet, while saluting the painter as a true representative of antiquity, had declared:

> *Tout passe, l'art robuste*
> *Seul a l'éternité.*

These words Whistler might well have echoed.

---

[1] In *Le Moniteur*, 18th November, 1864. On this period, cf. Louis Hautecoeur, *Littérature et Peinture en France*, 1942.

The Nocturnes

FORTUNATELY, in the 1870s Whistler abandoned his attempts to make his mark in classical and ideal painting. It was a correct decision, for this was not his proper genre; thus he decided to return to an appraisal of the world around him. This time he did not view Nature in the realistic manner of the 1850s or 1860s; his awareness of different artists and experiences of varied localities like the Pacific and the Normandy coast had helped him to change his outlook. Above all, he was eager to give a more radical turn to his vision of the modern world, nevertheless, one nurtured and refined by his belief in an ideal conception of art. Low-toned painting had always appealed to him, as may be seen from an early picture like *At the Piano* (Fig. 2), and already his first views of the Thames, of which the *Battersea Reach* (Fig. 9: Corcoran Gallery, Washington) is a good example, indicate his concern with the suggestion of atmosphere, a misty outline of buildings and a selective view of the scene. Then, too, in 1864 he had spoken of catching 'an effect of fog'.[1] There is little doubt, as well, that his study of the Japanese print (and perhaps of Canaletto, whom he greatly admired) had furthered his aim of painting a broad expanse of water depicted with unified tones.

The trend towards this new style may be seen in pictures like *Variations in Violet and Green* (Private collection, U.S.A.) and the *Variations in Pink and Grey: Chelsea* (Fig. 24: Freer Gallery, Washington), both of about 1870–1, but in neither of these transitional canvases are the figures quite blended into the composition; it is as if they are interlopers from one of his more Pre-Raphaelite works. In the Freer composition, the elegant figures also look ahead to those in the Cremorne Gardens series; a similar elegance of touch occurs in the dabs of pinkish coloured paint which are employed to represent the leaves and the sails of the boat.

The scarcity of precisely datable Nocturnes makes it hard to provide any exact chronology of his work in this genre. One is probably right in assuming that a picture like the *Nocturne Blue and Silver*, in the Freer Gallery, Washington, dates from the early 1870s. One factor which supports this contention is that Whistler has not transposed the scene into what might be termed its poetical equivalent; and we are very conscious that the site is a real one, namely, the embankment

[1] Letter to Fantin-Latour 3rd February, 1863. Library of Congress, Washington.

63

opposite Lindsey Gardens, where he lived; this sort of scene with ships with furled sails riding at anchor may be found in a contemporary photograph published by the Pennells.[1] Yet he was soon to abandon any attempt to secure too insistent a literalness in his subject matter, as well as the introduction of inappropriate figures; the rapid manner in which he moved away from this conception and mastered a genre which became so completely his own is demonstrated in the *Nocturne in Blue and Green: Chelsea* (Plate III), painted in 1871 for his friend and patron W. C. Alexander and now in the possession of the Misses Alexander.

This is one of the most beautiful of the early Nocturnes, radiant with the freshness which occurs when an artist realises that he has hit upon a style and a theme corresponding to his deepest needs. For the first time, Whistler obtained in his picture a unified surface made up of gentle but not static tones, seen on one plane, and this general unity is vivified in this particular instance by dots of colour used to indicate the presence of lights, a procedure already employed in some of the Valparaiso series. In this canvas Whistler implemented that conception of painting to which he had devoted some thought three years earlier and described in a letter to Fantin-Latour, when thanking him for the gift of two flower pictures. 'It seems to me', he wrote,[2] 'that colour ought to be, as it were, embroidered on the canvas, that is to say, the same colour ought to appear in the picture continually here and there, in the same way that a thread appears in an embroidery, and so should all the others, more or less according to their importance; in this way, the whole will form a harmony. Look how well the Japanese understood this. They never look for the contrast, on the contrary, they're after repetition.'

This arrangement of the picture so as to achieve a harmony may be seen in works like the *Nocturne in Blue and Silver: Cremorne Lights* of 1872 in the Tate Gallery, London, or the *Nocturne in Blue and Gold: Old Battersea Bridge* (Fig. 25: Tate Gallery) of about the same date; these also show that the river acted as a springboard for his imagination, and the presence of sprays of blossom in the former might suggest that the locality could as well be in the Orient as in Europe. Close in date to these pictures must come the *Harmony in Grey and Silver, Chelsea Wharf*, in the National Gallery, Washington, which was certainly painted prior to 1875 when it was exhibited at the Society of French Artists; this has the same russet colouring in the sails as appears in *Battersea Reach* (Fig. 9: Corcoran Gallery, Washington). It is also related to the *Nocturne in Grey and Silver, Chelsea Embankment, Winter*, in the Freer Gallery, Washington, though in this canvas the effects are slightly more blurred.

The title 'Nocturne' was not coined by Whistler himself, although its musical connotation clearly relates it to his use of the word 'Symphony', and, at first, such pictures were called 'moonlights'. However, according to Mrs Leyland and her son-in-law, Val Prinsep, F. R. Leyland, one of the artist's staunchest patrons and

---

[1] Pennell, I, opp. p. 108.
[2] Letter of 30th September, 1868. Library of Congress, Washington.

himself a passionate amateur musician, suggested the word 'Nocturne' for them.[1]
Whistler quickly took up the idea, writing to Leyland: 'I say I can't thank you too
much for the name "Nocturne" as a title for my moonlights. You have no idea
what an irritation it proves to the critics and consequent pleasure to me—besides
it is really charming and does so poetically say all I want to say and *no more* than I
wish.'[2] He was quite right; what he wanted to express in such pictures was the
visual impression of the scene in terms of low-pitched colours, arranged so as to
secure a decorative and evocative pattern. He made his position quite explicit in his
comment on the *Nocturne in Grey and Gold: Chelsea Snow* (Fig. 26), in the Fogg
Museum, Cambridge: 'I care nothing for the past, present, or future of the black
figure, placed there because the black was wanted at that spot. All that I know is
that my combination of grey and gold is the basis of the picture. Now this is
precisely what my friends cannot grasp.'[3]

Whistler's determination to bring out the decorative and the abstract qualities
in a picture is made absolutely clear in these words; they show that the emphasis
is to be placed on the pictorial element in a composition. This aspect of his approach,
one which has a particular appeal at the present time, may be discerned in two of
his most celebrated pictures—the *Nocturne in Black and Gold: The Falling Rocket*
(Plate IV), in the Institute of Arts, Detroit, and the *Nocturne in Black and Gold:
The Fire Wheel*, in the Tate Gallery, London, both of which date from 1874.
His intention in painting such pictures, as he explained during the course of the
famous 'Whistler versus Ruskin' case, was to produce 'an arrangement of line,
form and colour first, and I make use of any incident of it which shall bring about
a symmetrical result'.[4] The visual appeal is wonderfully conveyed—in those
balloons of red and green colour that disport themselves in a bluish-green sky.
In choosing to depict scenes of night illuminations, Whistler may be considered as
belonging to a tradition which comprised artists like Wright of Derby and Volaire,
though it is highly improbable that he ever turned to either for inspiration.

The Oriental affinities of his art are also recalled in the Nocturnes, of which one
of the most delicate and evanescent, so subtle are the tones, is the *Nocturne: Snow
Storm*, in the National Museum of Wales, Cardiff. It is an astonishing picture in
which the timelessness of the scene and the delicate interplay of the greys are truly
tinged with the Far Eastern spirit, so that we feel that we are being led into the
world of the Sung landscape painters. And it is in a painting like this that he
succeeded in expressing the essence of the exotic vision which tantalised him and
which answered to his own sensitive nature, rather than in the more overtly and
fancy dress, Oriental subject-paintings. This evocative picture is presumably
related to the *Nocturne in Brown and Gold: Chelsea Rags* and the *Nocturne in Grey*

---

[1] In the *Art Journal*, August, 1892, cited by Pennell, I, p. 166.
[2] Undated letter of the early 1870s; Pennell, I, p. 116.
[3] *The Gentle Art of Making Enemies*, p. 126.   [4] Pennell, I, p. 234.

and Gold: Chelsea Snow (Fig. 26), both in the Fogg Museum, Cambridge, the latter of which was painted in 1878. It is also probable that two of his most unusual and revolutionary Nocturnes—the *Nocturne: Westminster Palace*, in the John G. Johnson collection, Philadelphia, and the *Nocturne in Blue and Silver, Battersea Reach*, in the Isabella Stewart Gardner Museum, Boston, belong to the same period. These are splendid examples of Whistler's atmospheric painting, and a few touches of justly placed paint, as in the Gardner picture, suffice to indicate the faint outline of the craft sneaking its passage across the water.

Whistler's Nocturnes after Nature were not painted on the site, a method in any case impractical, but, in accordance with the principles laid down by Lecoq de Boisbaudran, he relied on memory. This may afford one explanation of their brilliantly selective character. He would make rough drawings while boating on the Thames or else, on other occasions, on his return home jot down a sketch of what he had seen. His reliance on memory is borne out by a story told by Way,[1] who recounts how when, walking along the road by the gardens of Chelsea Hospital, Whistler suddenly stopped 'and pointing to a group of buildings in the distance, an old public house at the corner of the road, with windows and shops showing golden lights through the gathering mist of the twilight, said, "Look!" As he did not seem to have anything to sketch or make notes on, I offered him my note-book. "No, no, be quiet", was the answer; and after a long pause he turned and walked back a few yards; then, with his back to the scene at which I was looking, he said, "Now see if I have learned it", and repeated a full description of the scene, even as one might repeat a poem one had learned by heart.' Nevertheless, Whistler may have made a drawing at home—namely, the sketch now at Glasgow University (Revillon Bequest), which is related to *Chelsea Rags* and *Chelsea Snow* (Fig. 26), both of about 1878, in the Fogg Museum, Cambridge, Mass.

Whistler's discovery of a congenial artistic form was matched by his care in finding a technique corresponding to his aims. Walter Greaves, who knew him well, pointed out[2] that 'the Nocturnes were mostly painted on very absorbent canvas, sometimes on panels, sometimes on bare brown holland, sized'. For the blue Nocturnes, the canvas was covered with a red ground or else a mahogany panel was chosen . . . 'the red forcing up the blues laid on it'. Others were done on 'practically a warm black'; for those pictures in which fireworks appear, a lead ground was chosen. Whistler's desire for a concordance of tone was stressed by his contention that if the night was grey, then the sky is grey and the water grey; therefore the canvas must be grey and, only once, in Greaves's memory, was a white ground employed; in fact, the ground for his Nocturnes, like the paper chosen for a pastel, was selected so as to match the prevailing tone of the picture he had in mind or of a colour which would give him

[1] *Memories of James McNeill Whistler the Artist*, 1912, pp. 67-8 repr. following p. 68.
[2] Pennell, I, pp. 164-5.

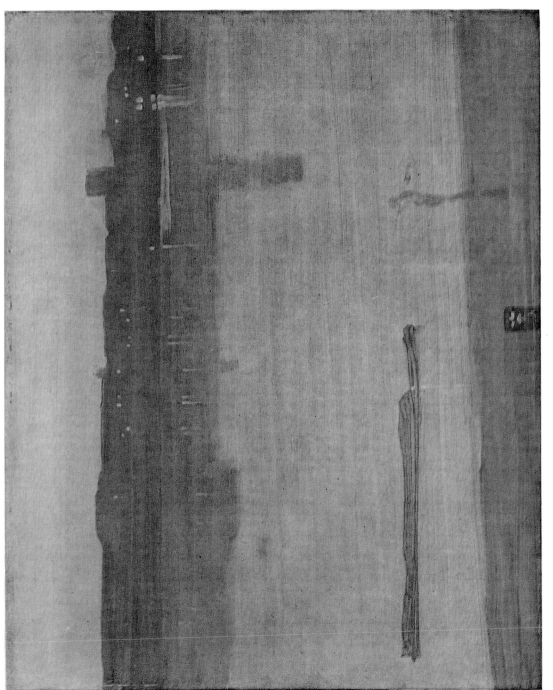

III. NOCTURNE IN BLUE AND GREEN: CHELSEA. Panel 19 x 23½ in. Signed with a butterfly and dated '71' (The Misses R. and J. Alexander, London).

that tone, not to save work, but to save disturbing, 'embarrassing' his canvas.

In such pictures the medium was composed of copal, mastic and turpentine; while the colours were arranged upon a palette, at the top of which were placed the pure colours, though more frequently, Greaves pointed out, pure colour was not used at all. Large quantities of the different tones of the dominant colour in the picture were mixed before work started, and so much of this medium used that Whistler called it a 'sauce'. After Whistler had arranged the colour scheme on the palette and prepared the 'sauce', the canvas or panel destined to receive it, although it may have been first of all placed on an easel, was often laid down on the floor so as to prevent the 'sauce', which was used liberally, from running off; the liquid colour was washed on to the composition and Whistler would lighten or darken the tone, as needs be, while working. In many Nocturnes, the entire expanse of the sky or the water, as may be seen even in reproduction, is rendered with great sweeps of the brush, and in exactly the right tone. 'How many times he made and wiped out that sweeping tone is another matter. When it was right, there it stayed.'[1] Owing to the unpredictable nature of his method, some Nocturnes were completed in a day, others were finished only after innumerable attempts; on occasion he would remove the colours from the palette and keep them on one side for the appropriate moment: and some of his pictures were put out in the garden or on the roof so as to dry more quickly.

Whistler's technical accomplishments are excellently illustrated in a series of four pictures of Cremorne Gardens in the Fogg Museum, Cambridge, the Metropolitan Museum, New York, and the Freer Gallery, Washington, respectively, which were probably painted before 1877 (when the Gardens were closed down) and which are connected with the Nocturnes. A particularly remarkable example of his use of what may be called without over-exaggeration the 'drip technique' is the truly astonishing *Cremorne Gardens No. 3*, in the Freer Gallery; to achieve his effects, which rely on a concentration of light upon the brightly illuminated portico in the gardens, the artist was quite prepared to shroud the left-hand portion of the composition in darkness; and in this portion, oblivious to any demands for 'finish' (the reproach levelled against him by Ruskin), the 'sauce' has been allowed to flow over the lighted portion of the canvas. The *Nocturne in Green and Gold: Cremorne Gardens, London, at Night No. 4*, in the Metropolitan Museum, New York, which is now in a poor state, is no less revolutionary by reason of its almost complete denial of colouristic possibilities and the reduction of light to a bare minimum; in fact, only a few areas are lighted at all and the figures themselves are indicated by means of summary dashes of pigment.

As a whole, this series brings out the remarkable variety of Whistler's art, within a relatively narrow compass; and in it he did not deny the introduction of an elegant note, apparent in the silhouetted figures who appear in the well-known

[1] Pennell, I, p. 165.

Cremorne Gardens No. 2 (Fig. 27), in the Metropolitan Museum, New York, rendered as if in a Kakemono. This is one of those pictures in which the artist has achieved his aims, presenting us with a sort of *fête galante* in contemporary terms, in which the wistful figures are somehow breathed on to the canvas. It contains such delicate passages as the almost ghostly man in green on the left and the subtly indicated chair, which, curiously enough, bears a resemblance to the sort of chair Seurat painted some years later. This happens to be one of Whistler's few pictures in which the arrangement of the figures in space and the arabesques they form are analogous to similar features in certain pictures by Toulouse-Lautrec, Bonnard and Vuillard; but the application of colour and its range are quite different from the ones these men used.

The care devoted to the Nocturnes underlines the fact that Whistler was not prepared to remain content with one solution alone, but that he was continually anxious to look about him for different, and more perfect, ways of perfecting his vision. He was not bound by adherence to any one specific method; his technique varied according to the subject in hand. He could spring surprises as in the *Nocturne, Blue and Silver, Bognor*, in the Freer Gallery, Washington, with its radiant blue in which, to quote George Moore, 'the waves curl white in the darkness, and figures are seen as in dreams; lights burn low, ships rock in the offing, and beyond them, lost in the night, a vague sense of illimitable sea'.[1] It is unexpected to find in this picture that, although painted prior to 1878, when it was shown at the Grosvenor Gallery, he has reverted to the more Courbet-like style of the 1860s; at the same time, its technique foreshadows that of the many small seascapes which date from the 1880s onwards.

Whistler was not the first painter to have tackled night scenes; such subjects had been previously explored by Elsheimer and Van der Neer in the seventeenth century, and, nearer his own time, by Augustus Egg and Jongkind, both of whom painted 'moonlights' in the 1850s, and, to some extent, he may be counted as an heir to the romantic tradition. But he was the first artist of his generation really to bring out the aesthetic content of the nocturnal world and, in deciding to interpret a great city at night and in evoking, as he did so successfully, its twilight hours, he plainly demonstrated his connection with modern sensibility. He touched a chord which a Baudelaire or a Poe had already sounded; and he might have echoed the narrator's words in the *Murders of the Rue Morgue* that 'it was a freak of fancy in my friends (for what else shall I call it?) to be enamoured of the Night for her own sake; and into this bizarrerie, as into all others, I quietly fell'. There is, indeed, something about the moment when day fades into night which accords with the mood, both romantic and pessimistic, of many of the creative spirits of the period; and who can forget the sad image of D. G. Rossetti, tortured by self-recriminations and problems, wandering through nocturnal London. This is the moment which arouses dreams and regrets; passions, too, as Baudelaire revealed in *Les Fleurs du Mal*.

[1] *Modern Painting*, 1893, p. 23.

22 SYMPHONY IN
BLUE AND PINK.

Oil on board, 18¼ ×
24 in. *About* 1868.
*Freer Gallery of Art,
Washington.*

23 VARIATIONS IN
BLUE AND GREEN.

Panel, 18½ × 24⅜ in.
About 1868. *Freer
Gallery of Art,
Washington.*

25 NOCTURNE IN BLUE AND GOLD: OLD BATTERSEA BRIDGE.

Canvas, 26¼ × 19¼ in. First exhibited in 1877, though painted

24 VARIATIONS IN PINK AND GREY: CHELSEA.

Canvas, 24⅝ × 16 in. About 1871. Butterfly signature.

Paradoxically, although Whistler never tried to convey a specific message in his Nocturnes and was intent only on exposing the artistic qualities inherent in night-fall, contemporary men of letters[1] responded to his pictures with considerable sympathy; although in the early days Henry James disapproved of Whistler's art, Wilde, Symons, Wratislaw and Henley were among the writers who found inspiration in the painter's novel subject-matter, seeing in them the expression of a mood corresponding to their own. At times, the purely descriptive character of such verse recalls Whistler's painting, as when, for example, Symons wrote:

> *The masts rise white to the stars,*
> *White on the night of the sky,*
> *Out of the water's night;*
> *And the stars lean down to them, white.*[2]

or when Wratislaw declared:

> *A mist on the darkened river*
> *Falls; on the rippled stream*
> *The yellow lights shake and quiver*
> *The red lights quiver and gleam.*[3]

At other times a special, more subjective twist was given to the river seen at night. In a remarkable poem, dedicated to Whistler, Henley wrote:

> *Under a stagnant sky,*
> *Gloom out of gloom uncoiling into gloom,*
> *The River, jaded and forlorn,*
> *Welters and wanders wearily—wretchedly—on;*
> *Yet in and out among the ribs*
> *Of the old skeleton bridge, as in the piles*
> *Of some dead lake-built city, full of skulls,*
> *Worm-worn, rat-riddled, mouldy with memories,*
> *Lingers to babble to a broken tune*
> *(Once, O, the unvoiced music of my heart):*
> *So melancholy a soliloquy*
> *It sounds as it might tell*
> *The secret of the unending grief-in-grain,*
> *The terror of Time and Change and Death,*
> *That wastes this floating, transitory world. . . .*[4]

[1] For an excellent account of the aesthetic writers in England at this time, see Albert J. Farmer, *Le mouvement esthétique et décadent en Angleterre (1873–1900)*, 1931.
[2] The poem, which is entitled 'Intermezzo: Venetian Nights' (1894), appeared in *London Nights* (1895). See *Poems*, Vol. I, 1924, p. 218.
[3] *On the Embankment*, in *Caprices*, 1893, p. 13.
[4] *Rhymes and Rhythms* (1885–1892), in *Poems*, 1921, pp. 135–6.

One might have expected Whistler to object to an interpretation of the River—his river, one might add—which has a curious foretaste of T. S. Eliot; but this was not so; on the contrary, he offered Henley one of his Nocturnes for use as a lithographic illustration for the poem when it appeared in *The London Garland*.[1] Perhaps he was right to have done so; the painterly qualities in the Nocturnes are pre-eminent, but the mood they undoubtedly suggest, one of melancholy and sobriety, can arouse a feeling not so different from that so finely captured by Henley.

The majority of the Nocturnes are exquisite pictures in their own right—daring, inventive and evocative. They succeed in transforming our view of a familiar scene so that after his vision the Thames can never be seen, at certain times of day or in certain seasons, without his pictures coming to mind. But he accomplished something even more striking; he created an artistic language, depending on the interplay of tonalities and creating a vision of space—which is his, and his alone. The sources which contributed to its making are digested, so that he provided a highly personal visual image; one which still exerts its poetry. And there is one other aspect about his concern with night that ought also to be remembered; namely, that many of his compatriots—Ryder, Blakelock, for instance—were also taken by nocturnal subjects, and, in this respect, Whistler is perhaps more American than generally suspected. Certain points of contact may also be observed between his work and that of Winslow Homer; for instance, the streaky passages of white-grey paint which this artist used to depict ice in a picture like the *Hound and Hunter*, in the National Gallery of Art, Washington, recalls Whistler's technique; and both shared a common love of the sea.[2]

[1] Pennell, II, p. 166.

[2] Mr Albert Ten Eyck Gardner in *Winslow Homer, American Artist*, 1961, has argued that Homer's visit to Paris in 1866–7, by bringing him into contact with Japanese art, radically altered his style. For a rather different view, see Lloyd Goodrich's review of this book in *The New York Times Book Review*, of 26th November, 1961, p. 7.

FIVE

The Portraits of the 1870s

WHISTLER'S experiments with the Nocturnes, his prints, his decorative enterprises and his active social life did not prevent him from devoting serious attention to the problems of portrait painting. From the 1870s onwards, it became one of his chief preoccupations, one which taxed his strength and ingenuity as he strove to live up to his ideal of perfection. In a sense, he had much to overcome, for he had to find a style which was viable within the self-imposed limitations of his colour range, and with the portrait, as with his other pictures, he mainly used low-toned colours. Thus he was rarely in a position to make, as it were, a diversion by catching the eye by a bravura passage, as did his fellow countryman Sargent.

Moreover, he was a painter who found it exceedingly difficult to build up a composition slowly, section by section; this was not his method at all; on the contrary, if dissatisfied he preferred to rub down a picture and virtually start from scratch. This practice was to prove as laborious for him as for the sitter. His aims were ambitious as well. He sought to provide a total image of the sitter, one which was harmonious and consistent in its details, and, at the same time, he tried to hint at the mysterious relationships which link a sitter, any sitter, to the external world and which reflect his inner life. Here the positive, even optimistic side of his nature broke through; the basis of his portrait-art was a conviction that individuality exists in all of us. And to accomplish his aim he had to provide an instantaneous statement which took account of the inner spark which fires the personality; and he had to catch that one moment of time when all the elements, which held his attention, were fused simultaneously in front of his eyes so that he could perceive their intimate and revealing meanings. Obviously, such an approach demanded exploration and prolonged contemplation; also many trials had to be surmounted before he could hit upon the propitious moment and the right blending of all the component parts.

He had painted a number of portraits in his youth, among them the *Self Portrait* (Fig. 1), in the Freer Gallery, Washington, and the *Portrait of Luke Ionides*, in the Cyril Ionides collection, Sussex; and the full-length pictures of Jo as the White Girl (Figs. 6, 12) were also portraits of a sort—but it was only in 1870 that he started work on a more comprehensive scale. Thus in the early 1870s he painted

71

his own portrait—the *Arrangement in Grey* (Frontispiece) in the Detroit Institute of Arts, which stylistically is close to his technique of the late 1860s.

His first major venture, however, was, appropriately, the famous portrait of his mother, the *Arrangement in Grey and Black No. 1* (Fig. 28), in the Louvre, on which he was certainly engaged by 1871. Exhibited at the Royal Academy in the following year, it became his most popular picture, and twenty years later, Watts could write to him that it was 'a real poem of the highest order, a most serene harmony, the impression of it remains with me like a strain of sweet and solemn music'.[1] Watts was right. It is a most tender picture in which the purity and integrity of Mrs Whistler are conveyed by means of the tightly constructed composition; and the concentration is emphasised by his placing the sitter in side view against an even-toned background, vivified by the presence of the rectangular shapes of the picture frames. She has an air of permanence about her. The cameo-like treatment of her head not only echoes the sort of approach found with Holbein, but bears a curious resemblance to certain contemporary American portraits. Such is the 'classical' note conveyed that P. G. Hamerton even maintained[2] that the artist may have picked up a hint for its composition from the figure of Agrippina in the Capitoline in Rome or from Canova's statue of Napoleon's mother at Chatsworth; although it is most unlikely that he tapped such sources, one knows what Hamerton means. Yet the picture is not entirely austere; this note is relieved by the soft strokes of paint on the curtain (surely a delicate cleaning would transform them into silver), which indicate a study of Velasquez.

Velasquez's shadow stands behind many of Whistler's portraits, and, as R. A. M. Stevenson neatly said: 'Truth is the introducer that bids these two men shake hands across several centuries.'[3] It is the memory of Velasquez which must account for the broad free handling of the hat in his *Arrangement in Grey and Black No. 2: Thomas Carlyle* (Plate V), in the City Art Gallery, Glasgow—the second of his major portraits. Carlyle had been persuaded to sit after Madame Emilie Venturi had taken him to see the artist's *Portrait of his Mother*, and the connections between the two pictures, both of which are conceived as profile portraits, is obvious enough. As always with Whistler, the execution presented great difficulties and Carlyle told William Allingham[4] in July, 1873, that the artist would scream out in an agonised tone: 'For God's sake don't move.' The head does not seem to have caused much hardship and is a lively piece of painting; it was the coat which gave the trouble and Whistler devoted endless attention to securing the tonal accuracy he wanted. But the finished result surely justified the pains taken. At what stage in the proceedings he did the pen and ink drawing[5] and the oil sketch of the head and shoulders in Haverford College, Pennsylvania, is not quite clear; if they were

[1] Letter of July 14th, 1891, in the University of Glasgow.   [2] Pennell, I, p. 169.
[3] *Velasquez*, original edition published 1895; new edition by T. Crombie and D. Sutton, 1962, p. 89.
[4] *A Diary*, ed. H. A. and D. Radford, 1907, p. 227.   [5] Pennell, I, facing p. 170.

preparatory to the final composition, as now seen, it would suggest that he found the pose itself easily enough; but they could have been executed simultaneously with work on the portrait; the oil sketch could conceivably have been painted subsequently.

One of Whistler's special gifts as a portrait painter was a flair for hitting upon a pose which suited the sitter. Thus he was often at his best in portraits of women and children, for whom he had a natural sympathy. His skill in this direction is illustrated in the celebrated *Harmony in Grey and Green: Miss Cicely Alexander* (Fig. 29), in the National Gallery, London. Here he adopted principles which are similar to those used with the Nocturnes; thus he prepared the setting in advance—and, as an indication of his desire to intervene decisively himself, he selected the muslin for the little girl's dress, tendering advice as to the way it should be made up. It was laundered under his supervision and he arranged where the bows and frills were to go; she was even posed on a special carpet of black and white tape. Then he started relentless work and the poor child was compelled to undergo over seventy sittings, but her tears of weariness in no way disturbed the artist—wrapped up in the creation of one of his true masterpieces.

Once again he acknowledged a debt to Velasquez—the *Portrait of the Infanta Margaret*, in the Louvre (which is no longer given to him), comes to mind—but this connection does not dampen the picture's personality. And it is one of those works in which his solicitude for the proper arrangement, for the improvement of 'Nature', paid off, and the nicely calculated decorative arrangement does not detract from the rendering of the girl's spirit—with its hint of a pout. He transformed the picture into a still-life, but one in which the outward movement of the leg, the curl of the muslin attached to the hat, the illusion that the two butterflies are fluttering, exclude heaviness. This is an extraordinarily cunning composition in which the almost uniform grey of the wall is relieved by the dark brown area of the dado and the strip of brown intersecting the grey, the discreet but in a sense bravura passage of the material, and the few flowers on the right; all this tones in with, and directs attention to, the delicious dress with its flounces and, as a lasting coquettish note, the ornament in her hair; as Mr James Laver charmingly wrote, 'the little girl herself is like some delicate white moth poised for an instant with faintly fluttering wings'.[1]

Whistler was also eager to paint the Alexanders' other daughters but, although various sketches in oil, pastel, chalk and pen and ink were done, the only portrait which nearly reached completion was the *Agnes Mary, Miss Alexander*, in the Tate Gallery. This is not one of his most successful pictures but, in spite of its unfinished state, and even perhaps because of it, it remains one of the most intriguing and significant of the early works. Previously, in the portraits of Jo, he had suggested

---

[1] Op. cit., p. 122. For a recent account of this picture, see Reginald Colby, 'Whistler's Controversial Masterpiece' in *Country Life*, cxxxii (2nd August), 1962, pp. 260–1.

an air of mystery and melancholy, hinting at deeper things, but now, for the first time, he really succeeded in conjuring up a sort of ghost-like atmosphere. A similar note stamps *The White Girl, No. 4* in the Fogg Museum, Cambridge, which was certainly painted before 1874 (when shown at the Pall Mall Gallery); in this picture he presents a vision, it is nothing less, which seems to enter the spectator's ken as does a wraith. It is as if he summons someone from another world. The girl stands there, almost trembling—rather insistent: as if she was the symbol of some half-forgotten crime. The disembodied effect is stressed by the fans which appear in the background and which are shown as if they were extraneous features. Although the picture (Fig. 18) was exhibited in the artist's lifetime, the right hand portion appears to be unfinished.

This was one side of Whistler's art as a portraitist, and one that gained ascendancy during the years. But he was not exclusively concerned with such almost supernatural painting at this stage. In the early 1870s, he undertook a number of important commissions for F. R. Leyland, the Liverpool shipowner and art collector, who asked him to paint his own portrait and those of his wife and their four children. As his patron had not yet acquired his London residence, Whistler was compelled to pay various visits to the Leylands' country house, Speke Hall, near Liverpool, and he made several charming etchings of this place (p. 75).

The *Arrangement in Black: F. R. Leyland* (Fig. 31) of 1873, in the Freer Gallery, Washington, was the first full-length male portrait he had attempted; and its execution was not without its problems; Leyland himself remembered the difficulty Whistler faced when attempting to give the legs their correct stance. Once more, he summoned Velasquez to his aid, and the debt to the Spanish master is clear enough; and it is fair to recall that the various *pentimenti* in many of the great Spaniard's full-length portraits show that he too had found the depiction of this sort of pose extremely trying. One problem which challenges the portrait painter is the presentation of the whole figure so that it naturally inhabits the space allotted to it and does not take on the appearance of a playing card—as do so many seventeenth-century journeyman portraits. Whistler succeeded in this brilliantly realised portrait; on this occasion, as on many subsequent ones, he adapted the silhouette form previously used for the seated portraits.

Two oil sketches of Leyland also exist, but it is by no means certain where they fit in. One small sketch, formerly with Messrs P. and D. Colnaghi, London, represents Leyland in a short coat with his right hand held up to his beard while leaning on a cane held in his left hand; this could have been an independent study, but it might have been a try-out for the formal portrait. The other sketch, once in Charles Conder's possession, which is closer to the Freer picture, might suggest that, although finding the pose he wanted without much difficulty (as was usual with him), some alterations did occur; for instance, the background of a dado with a wall cut by a single upright line was suppressed in favour of a dark background and a lighter coloured floor. He also did a drawing of Leyland now in the Metropolitan Museum, New York.

Whether or not the artist was in love with Leyland's wife, as is sometimes alleged, will probably never be known. He certainly nourished a warm sentiment for her; she must have been one of the first ladies with a touch of the *grande dame* about her (although, of course, she was not in Society) with whom he was on close terms. The strength of his feeling for the Leyland family certainly transpires from

SPEKE HALL
Etching, 8¼ × 5⅞ in. Signed and inscribed 'Whistler 1870 Speke Hall'. British Museum, London.

an undated letter to Mrs Leyland in which he declared that: 'It is natural enough that utter desolation should set in now that you all have taken your departure and everything like life has gone with you—and desolation it accordingly is.'[1] It is hardly surprising that among his early portraits of women, hers (Fig. 32) should be so outstanding. For one thing, the pose is both telling and unusual. She is presented neither in full face nor in true profile, but with her back to the spectator; and her features, owing to their relationship to the body, take on an air of almost disdainful beauty. Then she is extraordinarily elegant, but not in a *mondain* sense; the garments she wears have an aesthetic touch about them. She does not wear

[1] Undated letter, Christmas (1871?). Library of Congress, Washington.

formal clothes, but is dressed in a flowing loose gown of pink and white chiffon; the rosettes of a deeper shade serve to set off the appeal of her reddish hair. Her hands have the distinction found in Van Dyck. The decorative effect—that of a beautiful woman in her intimacy—is heightened by the sprays of almond blossom and by the dotted and patterned matting, which, although placed at some distance from the rose-tinted wall with its low dado, seem to blend with the background itself. In this picture the use of dotted matting is intriguing for another reason; it anticipates the sort of decorative effects found in the portraits of the Austrian *Art Nouveau* painter, Gustav Klimt.[1]

Whistler's response to feminine charm was a constant element in his pictures, but he avoided the cloying sweetness of the typical Salon or Academy painter. He knew when to be astringent or severe and, in such works, his love of darker tonalities was given full rein. Thus in the *Arrangement in Black No. 2: Portrait of Mrs Huth*, in the collection of Lord Cowdray, the composition arises out of a juxtaposition of blacks and greys. His skill in placing a full-length figure in an upright narrow canvas is especially well shown in this portrait; Mrs Huth's dress sweeps the floor with an almost curvilinear movement, which again hints at his relationship to *Art Nouveau*. And it remains a touching picture of withdrawal, suggestive, in this respect, of the sitter's delight in a private world. His sympathy for this same sort of pose is equally apparent in the portrait, *Arrangement in Black and Brown: Rosa Corder*, in the Frick collection, New York, in which he captured the particular charm, as Ellen Terry said, of 'one of those plain beautiful women who are so far more attractive than some of the pretty ones'.[2] And he did so by giving her features that cameo-like treatment he favoured and arranging the folds of her dress in a way suggestive of a Greek terra-cotta; hers is an elegance which gains through its very discretion. Now, however, the portrait has become dark: yet the subtlety of treatment is evident in the brown hat held in her hand; this detail again recalls Velasquez.

The portraits of the 1870s demonstrate Whistler's technical skill. Sometimes he would rely on shadow painting to attain the effect wanted; and in the lively full-length *Harmony in Flesh Colour and Black: Mrs Louise Jopling* (Fig. 34; Birnie Philip Bequest, Glasgow), a broad sweep of the brush—the sort of sweep used in the Nocturnes—suffices to indicate the bustle's whereabouts; it is by implication, not by finished painting, that he makes his point. This sense for atmosphere and for placing a figure in a background which conjures up the right setting, without actually revealing anything, is noticeable in the *Arrangement in Black and Brown: Fur Jacket*, in the Worcester Art Museum, Mass., which was shown at the Grosvenor Gallery in 1877. In this, although it was finished enough for

---

[1] Klimt himself seems to have been influenced by Whistler: see a picture of a *Dame am Kamin*, before 1900 in the Osterreichische Galerie, Vienna.

[2] Op cit., p. 282.

26 Nocturne in Grey and Gold: Chelsea Snow.
Canvas, $17\frac{1}{2} \times 24$ *in. Fogg Art Museum, Cambridge, Mass.*

27 Cremorne Gardens No. 2.
Canvas, $27 \times 53\frac{5}{8}$ *in. About 1875. Metropolitan Museum of Art, New York.*

28 ARRANGEMENT IN GREY AND BLACK No. 1: THE ARTIST'S MOTHER.
Canvas, 56 × 64 in. First exhibited in 1872. Louvre, Paris.

exhibition purposes, the bottom portion relies for its readability on suggestion, carried out by means of shadow painting; the effect heightens the impression, as the Pennells said, of 'the pale beautiful face [that] looks out, like a flower, from the depths of the background'.[1]

For modern eyes it is no less intriguing to find in the *Arrangement in Yellow and Grey: Effie Deans* of 1876, in the Rijksmuseum, Amsterdam, that the paint has been allowed to drip over the lower portion of the canvas. This picture is not a portrait proper, but a composition on a literary theme, and he took as his subject the line from Scott's *The Heart of Midlothian:* 'She sunk her head upon her hand and remained seemingly unconscious as a statue.' (The other two pictures on literary themes, the *Annabel Lee* and the *Ariel*, are both at Glasgow.) But he could define when he found, or felt, it to be necessary; such definition may be seen in the very stylish *Arrangement in Black and White No. 1: The Young American* (Fig. 33), in the Freer Gallery, Washington, exhibited at the Grosvenor Gallery in 1878, where his delight in the accentuation of the female form, occasioned by her tight dress, made him produce a direct dashing portrait; this possesses the sort of *brio* which many of his clients would have admired if he had been willing to use it in his portraits of them.

Whistler was interested in the stage during the 1870s; he often went to the theatre and took part in amateur theatricals. Also, he tried his hand at painting the portraits of two theatrical personalities. In about 1878 he invited the child actress, Connie Gilchrist, who was appearing at the Gaiety Theatre as a skipping rope dancer, to pose for him; this was thus another indication of his interest in children and adolescence, which became more insistent over the years. The picture which resulted, now in the Metropolitan Museum, New York, is, for him, a daring venture; in contrast to the majority of his portraits which represent a sitter in repose, she is depicted in movement, actually manipulating her rope and skipping.

It is not one of his most successful ventures and, not surprisingly, seems to have dissatisfied him: the Pennells maintained[2] that the long line swept down the outline of the figure indicated his intention of making further alterations to it; nevertheless, it has a certain appeal; the gentle folds of the curtain, serving as a brown grey background, act so as to project her ghostlike wistful figure, while the whiteness of her face (the expression is almost drained) is brought out by the red handles of the rope and the white grey tones of her bootees. Some light on his methods is afforded by the fact that the pen and ink drawing of her in the British Museum was apparently executed while he was in the throes of painting this portrait. In another portrait of her in the Birnie Philip Bequest, Glasgow, which, in view of her age, presumably, dates from the same period, the technique announces the looser manner of the later portraits while the green colours are lighter than usually found at this period.

[1] Pennell, I, p. 201. [2] Pennell, I, p. 202.

When Whistler saw the famous actor Henry Irving in the role of Philip II in Tennyson's play, *Queen Mary*, he was so taken by his performance that he prevailed upon the actor to sit to him wearing his theatrical costume. For him, the chance was too good to be missed; Irving was wearing an outfit which brought to mind the figures and costumes painted by his revered master, Velasquez; in fact, he was so delighted by the subject that he executed two very free etchings of the sitter, which relate to the earlier, not to the later, version of the portrait; moreover, it was one of the rare occasions when the artist tackled the same subject in another medium.

At the start he made good progress with the portrait and Alan Cole, visiting his studio in May, 1876, found him 'quite madly enthusiastic about his power of painting such full-lengths in two sittings or so'.[1] Yet Whistler proved to be over-optimistic and work on the portrait petered out. Nevertheless, it was certainly sufficiently advanced to be placed on exhibition, duly appearing at the Grosvenor Gallery in 1877 as *Arrangement in Black No. 3: Sir Henry Irving in the Character of Philip II of Spain in Tennyson's Queen Mary*. However, the artist did not consider the picture finished and, in the summer of 1885, he invited Irving to come and see the *Arrangement in Black: Pablo de Sarasate* (Fig. 43), in the Carnegie Institute, Pittsburgh, then on view at the Society of British Artists exhibition: 'Let that show you what I meant your portrait to be and then arrange with me for a day or two in my new studio.'[2]

The reproduction in Duret's volume is of the picture as it presumably looked after the sittings in 1876: a comparison of the two versions shows that he was able to take it further. As Mr McLaren Young has pointed out: 'It shows that many changes were made later: there is no chain, no garter, the plume is much larger, and—most striking of all—the part of the cloak on the left is thrown behind the shoulder. Irving must therefore have accepted Whistler's invitation and posed for him again in about 1885. The absence of a signature, however, suggests that he did not do so for as long as Whistler wished.'[3] The finished work (Fig. 45) is striking, all the same; it is painted with a rather dry pigment with an emphasis on greys and yellows, though dashes of red occur in the handling of the face. It is not a picture which yields to the first inspection and only after some study does its vivacity become apparent. It demonstrates that when in form he could prove a master of a sort of modern 'state portrait', and of a type which had almost died out in his time, at any rate, in the hands of a true artist.

Enough has been said to show that Whistler during the decade 1870–1880 had evolved a varied and impressive manner of portrait painting. The elements which had gone to make it are no less clear: *Japonaiserie*, to some extent Pre-Raphaelitism, and Velasquez. On the last count, he outstripped a French painter like Carolus-Duran, whose *La Dame au Gant* of 1869 in the Louvre provides an

---

[1] Pennell, I, p. 199.   [2] Cited by Laurence Irving, *Henry Irving*, 1951, p. 274.
[3] *Whistler Catalogue (Arts Council)*, 1960, p. 59.

excellent illustration of the way in which a competent painter could make use of the Spanish master's findings. Inevitably, certain points of contact link the two men, but the comparison is illuminating in so far as it illustrates the personal way in which Whistler manipulated his own sense of space and his feeling for the nuances of colour. The extent to which Whistler was aware of current trends in Paris during the late 1860s and 1870s is hard to define, and scant assistance is provided by the published or unpublished documents relating to him. As he was often in Paris during this period and kept up his connection with French circles, one may assume that he saw much of what was going on, though whether or not it was to his taste is more debatable. For instance, he was in Paris in 1867 when Fantin-Latour's *Portrait of Manet* (Art Institute, Chicago) was shown at the Salon, but although certain similarities may be detected between their works, the resemblance is no more than superficial. It seems to be clear enough that he turned his back on most of his French contemporaries, making no effort to follow the major men. For in the 1870s Cézanne painted the *Portrait of Victor Chocquet* (Lord Rothschild, Cambridge), Renoir the *Portrait of Mme Henriot* (Mr and Mrs David Levy, New York), and Manet *Skating*, 1877 (Maurice Wertheim collection, New York).

There was no reason that he should have followed in their directions and what, to later generations, might seem a wilful dismissal of 'modernism' on his part arose from his own preoccupations. In fact, in order to appreciate his portraiture properly one has to accept the fact that Impressionism (with which is included, for the sake of convenience, the art of Manet), although representing much that was best in nineteenth-century French art, was not mandatory on a painter; he could have his own vision and one not necessarily in accord with the Impressionist principles. In other words, there was room for more than one vision at this period (as, indeed, at others), and, while in no way underrating the radiant contribution of the Impressionists, one may also claim that pleasure may be derived from that handful of portraits from the 1870s in which Whistler demonstrated his independence of the *avant garde* trend; in these he revealed the charms of a method which relied on muted colours and on the indirect suggestions of the depth of human personality.

❦ SIX ❦

The Decorator

THE second half of the last century witnessed a serious attempt to alter the scope of interior decoration and to introduce a new and 'modern' spirit into design. These ideas were in the air out of a much needed reaction against the muddled and eclectic styles in the decorative arts so disastrously revealed at the International Exhibition of 1851. In their various ways, Pugin and Cole, among others, had already tried to discover a more rewarding and artistic approach to these problems, and in 1861 this trend received practical expression with the foundation of the firm of Morris, Marshall, Faulkner and Co. This composite team effort engaged the services not only of William Morris himself but of D. G. Rossetti, Ford Madox Brown, Edward Burne-Jones, Philip Webb, Peter Paul Marshall and Charles J. Faulkner. The aims advanced by these men were large and ambitious and the firm's prospectus claimed that artistic supervision 'can alone bring about harmony between the various parts of a successful work'.[1]

Although this harmony was mainly seen in terms of a return to mediaevalism, their conceptions were not so different from Whistler's; in fact, several of the cabinets produced by the Morris firm are rather like the cabinet Whistler produced in collaboration with Godwin. Yet his contribution to the revolution then slowly taking place is only now being realised: and his opinions made him an undoubted precursor of much modern design. His belief that the artist ought to adopt a sort of universal attitude to the arts made it quite logical for him to maintain that his own pictures should be connected with their setting. He saw them as fitting into an ensemble, telling the Pennells that 'the painter must also make of the wall upon which his work hung, the room containing it, the whole house, a Harmony, a Symphony, an Arrangement, as perfect as the picture or print which became a part of it'.[2]

Whistler's theories on decoration owed much to the example and influence of his friend E. W. Godwin, and, like this designer, he cared for simplicity and lightness; in this connection, one ought also to remember that Whistler, as an American, came from a country which had produced the Shaker furniture in

[1] See *Morris and Company 1861–1940* (Arts Council), 1961. Introduction p. 5.
[2] *Journal*, p. 299.

which these qualities were uppermost. At first, he experimented in his own house; only later did he undertake designs for a number of friends. His first house in Chelsea, which he took in 1863, was decorated in the Oriental taste, with fans, screens and Blue and White China. A similar Oriental note was struck in his second home in the district, No. 2 Lindsey Row (now 96 Cheyne Walk), into which he moved in 1867.

At this distance of time, any precise reconstruction of its appearance is difficult, but Miss Cicely Alexander, when sitting for her portrait, recalled that the artist was in the throes of decorating the staircase: 'It was', she said, 'to have a dado of gold, and it was all done in gold leaf, and laid on by himself, I believe.'[1] This was a task which caused him some trouble as he had difficulty in matching the gold shade required. He also seems to have painted flowers on the dado of the staircase, while a ship with spread sails appeared on the panels in the hall. One innovation, due to Whistler, was the use of plain distemper for the walls: this process (which went back to the practice of the eighteenth century) was inexpensive and in no way distracted the attention from the pictures.

The drawing room was treated in flesh colour and yellow (the last was possibly derived from the Japanese print in which yellow is a special feature) while his painting room was done up in black and grey: this, according to the Pennells, served as the background to pictures like the portraits of his mother, Carlyle and Miss Cicely Alexander. On the other hand, for the background of Mrs Leyland's portrait, he turned to the colour scheme of the drawing room, and her dress was supposed to harmonise with the flesh colour of the walls; the matting which replaced the Oriental rugs which had originally covered the floor also appears in this picture.

During the 1870s, Whistler enjoyed several opportunities to try out his hand at decorative schemes. In 1873 Sir Henry Cole (whose portrait he painted) invited him to submit a project for the decoration then being planned for the central gallery of the South Kensington Museum (the Victoria and Albert Museum) of which Cole was then the Director. Although a cartoon was apparently prepared in the studio provided for Whistler's use in the Museum, the mosaic was never actually carried out; but some idea of what it might have looked like can be gained from the charming pastel on brown paper, sometimes called the *Gold Girl*, in the collection of Mrs J. L. Neame, Jersey; this represents a girl with a parasol and is Japanese in flavour.

Whistler could have been sidetracked into such schemes, perhaps to the detriment of his other work. Indeed in the same year, W. C. Alexander, one of his most discerning patrons and himself a collector of Oriental art, who had just acquired Aubrey House in Campden Hill, Kensington, decided to redecorate

[1] Pennell, I, p. 174. A drawing of three ships with sails, evidently connected with this decoration, is in the Birnie Philip Bequest, Glasgow.

the interior. Whistler helped him by sketching out a few ideas which are embodied in the four colour schemes for the dining room (now in the Birnie Philip Bequest, Glasgow), which are both charming and harmonious owing to their use of blue and gold. These plans did not come to fruition, although he does seem to have executed a 'harmony in white' for the drawing room, which was subsequently replaced by an arrangement of Oriental tapestries. At the same time, for the dining room, he seems to have concerned himself, not only with suggesting how it should be painted, but with the design for a sideboard. The pen and ink sketches at Glasgow demonstrate that his aim was to create a simplified functional style, one which is clearly related to the design of those pieces made by Godwin for the house he lived in with Ellen Terry. They also show the influence on him of Oriental furniture.

His most considerable opportunity as a decorator came in 1876. Some years previously, his friend and patron, F. R. Leyland, had acquired a new London home, 49 Prince's Gate, in which he intended to hang his important collection of Italian Renaissance paintings, which included works by Botticelli and Crivelli, as well as his group of modern English pictures by Rossetti, Burne-Jones, Albert Moore and others. In order to give character to the house, which became one of the main 'art houses' of the period, he employed Norman Shaw, assisted by Jeckyll, to make various interior alterations; thus three living rooms were interconnecting, being divided by screens reminiscent of a church at Bois-le-Duc, and the gilded late eighteenth century staircase from Northumberland House was also installed. As a close, even intimate friend of the family, it was perfectly natural for Whistler to have been consulted about the decorations, and that he should have been asked to undertake some work there.[1] His first foothold was in the hall. And on 24th March, 1876, Alan Cole noted that he had 'seen Whistler's colouring of the Hall—very delicate cocoa colour and gold—successful'.[2] Cole is presumably referring to the panels of the staircase which are now in the Freer Gallery, Washington; these imitate aventurine lacquer and are decorated with small floral patterns in pale pink and white, rather Japanese in style. It is also possible, as Mr McLaren Young has suggested,[3] that the design for a staircase, which is on a sheet of notepaper, embossed F. R. L. (F. R. Leyland), may represent an idea connected with its decoration.

This was only a beginning; gradually he moved into the dining room. For this room, Jeckyll had designed a Jacobean pendant ceiling in which the pendants themselves were to serve as gas fittings; he had also put in a series of walnut shelves, fitted with brown Cordova leather decorated with small flowers, which were to house Leyland's important collection of Blue and White. This material

---

[1] For a detailed account of this decoration, see Peter Ferriday, 'The Peacock Room', in the *Architectural Review*, cxxv (1959), pp. 407–14.

[2] Pennell, I, p. 203.   [3] *Whistler Catalogue*, p. 90.

was also used to cover the walls. Space was left over the mantel for Whistler's
La Princesse du Pays de la Porcelaine, which the collector already owned, and
further room was available at the opposite end to accommodate other pictures
by Burne-Jones and Whistler. Understandably Whistler was anxious to see his
Three Figures, Pink and Grey included in the arrangement; this subject would
seem to link up with the picture which, according to W. M. Rossetti,[1] he was
painting for Leyland in 1867. The painter was also responsible for the design of
the sideboard, though when this was executed is not clear. However, in April,
1876, he was brought into the proceedings generally when Mrs Leyland told
him that 'Jeckyll writes what colour to do the doors and windows in the dining
room . . . I wish you would give him your ideas'.[2]

Little imagination is required to conjure up the scene in which the anxious
and good-natured patron consulted the man of taste. Leyland apparently fell in
with Whistler's suggestions concerning various aspects of the room; the artist
felt that the red border of the rug and the red flowers in the leather, which were
painted, not embossed, killed the tones in his own painting. Permission was
given to paint the flowers on the leather yellow and gold; Whistler was still
dissatisfied and Leyland, then extremely occupied with the problems occasioned
by the entry of the Leyland Line into the Atlantic trade, allowed him to make
further alterations on his own.

Some idea of the changes then taking place may be gleaned from an article in
the September issue of *The Academy*, which revealed that a clear peacock pattern
was not yet evolved, though a liberal use of gold paint on the leather was noticeable:
the pattern of the leather had been 'modified and enriched by the introduction of a
fair primrose tint into the flowers patterned upon the deep ground of gold'. In
forwarding this notice to Leyland, Whistler declared: '*Mon cher* Baron—*Je suis
content de moi!* The dining room is really alive with beauty—brilliant and gorgeous
while at the same time delicate and refined to the last degree. I have *at last* managed
to carry out thoroughly the plan of decoration I have formed—and I assure you,
you can have no more idea of the ensemble in its perfection, gathered from what
you last saw on the walls, than you could have of a complete opera, judging from
a third finger exercise! *Voila*—But don't come up yet—I have not yet quite
done—and you mustn't see it till the last touch is on . . .' In the same letter,
Whistler acknowledged the appeal of Jeckyll's work in the dining room: 'If there
be any quality whatever in my decoration, it is doubtless due to the inspiration
I may have received from the graceful proportions and lovely lines about me.'[3]

The sequence of events in the dining room remains somewhat obscure. Yet it
would appear that Whistler, having been given his head, postponed his trip to
Venice and began work all over again: the Peacock Room, as we know it today,

---

[1] Pennell, I, p. 149. [2] Cited by P. Ferriday, p. 412.
[3] Cited by P. Ferriday, op. cit., p. 412.

was now in the process of creation. By November the *Morning Post* carried a notice of the decoration and in a letter to Mrs Leyland, written before Christmas, he told her that: 'The dining room, however, I engage will be finished this week. It is something quite wonderful and I am extremely proud of it. As a decoration it is thoroughly new and most gorgeous though refined. Tell Freddie that I think it will be a large sum but even then barely pays for the work.'[1] By February of the new year, the work was finished. The stories of Whistler's behaviour over the room are too familiar to require repetition. But his conduct was astonishing on any account; it was surely unpardonable to have entertained so freely in another man's house; to have unleashed publicity about it; and even to have issued a pamphlet entitled 'Harmony in Blue and Gold: The Peacock Room', which provided a description of the colour scheme and the use of the peacock motif in the room.

Obscurity also reigns about the actual way in which he set about the decoration; there is some discrepancy between what he said and the available evidence concerning the decorations. Whistler's own words to the Pennells were that: 'I just painted as I went on, without design or sketch—it grew as I painted. And towards the end I reached such a point of perfection—putting in every touch with such freedom—that when I came round to the corner where I had started, why, I had to paint part of it over again, or the difference would have been too marked. And the harmony in blue and gold developing, you know, I forgot everything in my joy in it!'[2] This is all very well as far as it goes; undoubtedly to some extent Whistler was carried away in the excitement of the work, but it is not, perhaps, an altogether accurate account of what took place; indeed the design may have been more premeditated than appears from his statement. For one thing, he had thought of possibly decorating in this way a room at Aubrey House, but the project had been turned down.

Moreover, what of the sketches of the south wall of the Leyland room and the three shutters that are to be found in a notebook at Glasgow, and the other, rather similar, drawings reproduced by the Pennells? The Glasgow drawings, for instance, were they made in order to accompany a verbal description given to Leyland (as Mr McLaren Young has suggested)[3] or did he formulate some of his ideas prior to actually carrying out the design? The fact of the matter is that he does seem to have made a preliminary sketch; this is the remarkable sketch in watercolour, heightened with white, in the Birnie Philip Bequest at Glasgow; with its strongly Oriental touch, rather reminiscent of a Hokusai drawing, and its drips of paint, this affords evidence that the decorations were based on some preliminary studies.

Whatever means led to the creation of the room, and however much it enraged

[1] Undated letter (presumably 1876), Library of Congress, Washington.
[2] Pennell, I, p. 204.   [3] *Whistler Catalogue*, p. 91.

29 HARMONY IN GREY AND
GREEN: MISS CICELY
ALEXANDER.

Canvas, 74 × 39 in.
Butterfly signature. About 1872–
74. National Gallery, London.

30 THE GUITAR PLAYER.

Drypoint, 10⅞ × 7 in. Messrs
P. and D. Colnaghi, London.

31 ARRANGEMENT IN BLACK:
F. R. LEYLAND.
*Canvas, 75⅞ × 36⅛ in. 1873. First
exhibited in 1874. Freer Gallery of Art,
Washington.*

32 SYMPHONY IN FLESH COLOUR AND PINK:
MRS F. R. LEYLAND.
*Canvas, 82½ × 36½ in. Butterfly signature.
1873. First exhibited in 1874. Frick
Collection, New York.*

Leyland, it was one of the most extraordinary pieces of decoration ever to have been executed in England; as an example of exotic design, it is comparable to the interior of the Royal Pavilion at Brighton designed by John Nash. Incidentally, the dining room in the Pavilion contains peacocks. The room, now in the Freer Gallery, Washington, looks very different from the sort of simplified interior Whistler advocated. This was partly due to the actual design of the room, with its low-hanging pendants, its innumerable shelves and the proportion generally. In fact, photographs are apt to give the impression that the room is rather dowdy and even frowsty; but this impression is not confirmed by careful inspection; on the contrary, the blue-green colour produces a relatively cheerful impression—and so do the splendid gold panels in the middle of the wall opposite the door. In general, the decoration strikes a light note, and the ceiling adds to the richness of the effects. Above all, the decoration is carried by the gorgeous peacocks, painted in blue on gold shutters; these are boldly and brilliantly decorative (Fig. 35).

The use of the peacock motif was not unusual at this time; it can be found in a wallpaper designed by Godwin in 1876 and in Albert Moore's work;[1] Mintons produced a model of one in 1876 and Rossetti kept such a bird in his Chelsea garden, much to the annoyance of the neighbours, and for Whistler, as well, it would have possessed the Oriental connotation he favoured. The actual spatial disposition of the room presents certain comparisons[2] with the *Art Nouveau* style, the start of which it antedates; thus the curvilinear sweep of the peacocks with their delicate elegance brings to mind a typical *Art Nouveau* façade like Endell's Elvira atelier of 1897 in Vienna. The relationship with this international style is also suggested in the curious and rather unpleasant caricature of Leyland as the *Gold Scab*; this represents the luckless Leyland, one of the chief creditors at the artist's bankruptcy in 1879, as a hideous peacock playing the piano and sitting on the White House, Chelsea!

Unfortunately, much of the evidence which would contribute to an assessment of Whistler's rôle as a decorator in the 1870s is no longer available; for instance the rooms he designed for Sarasate and other friends are no more. Nevertheless, his reputation as a designer was considerable; it was sufficiently well established for him to be entrusted with the execution of a frieze for the Grosvenor Gallery, the headquarters of the new aesthetic movement, which was founded by Sir Coutts Lindsay in 1877. Although this no longer exists, some idea of its appear-

[1] He painted a fresco of peacocks for Frederick Lehmann's house in Berkeley Square in 1872. See A. L. Baldry, op. cit., p. 41.

[2] Whistler himself, however, was not prepared to accept any connection between his work and *Art Nouveau*. The Pennells recalled how when Lavery attempted to define '*L'Art Nouveau*, the precursor of the Isms and Ists', Whistler 'would hear of no definition. "There is—there can be—no *Art Nouveau*—there is only Art!" ' *Journal*, p. 73.

ance transpires from Walter Crane's description; he stated that it represented 'the phases of the moon, on the coved ceiling of the West Gallery, which has disappeared since its conversion into the Aeolian Hall, with stars on a subdued blue ground, the moon and the stars being brought out in silver, the frieze being divided into panels by the supports of the glass roof'.[1] It was, therefore, a sort of variant on a Nocturne.

Rather more information survives about another decorative venture in which the artist participated; this is the room on which he collaborated with E. W. Godwin and which was shown in the 1878 Paris International Exhibition. Happily a full account of it was given by the correspondent in the *American Architect and Building News* (27th July, 1878) under the title of the 'Primrose Room'; this is worth quoting *in extenso* since it conjures up the sort of experiment in interior design then taking place. According to this writer, the artist himself called the room a 'Harmony in Yellow and Gold'. He stated that 'outside a yellow wall is built up a chimney piece and cabinet in one of which the wood, like all the wood in the room, is a curiously light yellow mahogany. . . . The fireplace is flush with the front of the cabinet, the front panelled in gilt bars below the shelf and cornice, inclosing tiles of pale sulphur, above the shelf, a cupboard, with clear glass and triangular open niches at either side, holding bits of Kaga porcelain, chosen for the yellowishness of the red, which is a characteristic of that ware; the frame of the grate brass; the rails in polished steel; the fender the same. Yellow on yellow, gold on gold, everywhere. The peacock reappears, the eyes and the breast feathers of him, but whereas in Prince's Gate it was always blue on gold, or gold on blue, here the feather is all gold, boldly and softly laid on a gold-tinted wall. The feet to the table-legs are tipped with brass, and rest on a yellowish brown velvet rug. Chairs and sofas are covered with yellow, pure rich yellow velvet, darker in shade than the yellow of the wall, and edged with yellow fringe. The framework of the sofa has a hint of the Japanese influence, which faintly, but only faintly, suggests itself all through the room. Its latticework back and wheel-patterned ends might pass for bamboo; the carpentry is as light as if the long fingers of a saffron-faced artist had coaxed it into shape.'[2]

Beside this description, which conjures up an astonishing vision, there exists a photograph of the stand in the show (Fig. 36) and of the cabinet decorated with painted panels. The cabinet, which is close in style to the sideboard projected for Leyland, was designed by Godwin, and Whistler was responsible for the painting on it: in the view of the *Magazine of Art*, the Butterfly Suite was 'slight for every-day use'.[3] The furniture was exhibited by William Watts of 21 Grafton Street, Gower Street, London, a firm which went out of existence in the 1880s. In

[1] Pennell, I, p. 212. A similar account appears in Crane's *An Artist's Reminiscences*, 1907, p. 175.
[2] Pennell, I, p. 219–20.
[3] 1878, Vol. I, p. 116. Cited by Elizabeth Aslin, *19th-Century English Furniture*, 1962, p. 64.

addition, during the 1870s, Whistler designed a great screen in blue with a gold moon; this had originally been destined for Leyland, but, presumably owing to the quarrel, the artist was left with it on his hands; he kept it with him over the years and it can be seen in photographs of his studio taken in the 1890s. Now, somewhat battered, it is in the Birnie Philip Bequest, Glasgow.

The collaboration with Godwin was fruitful. It was Godwin who in 1878 designed the famous White House in Tite Street, Chelsea; one may probably assume that the artist played a large part in its formulation. Once again an attempt was made to give practical expression to Whistler's ideas on colour harmonies; the walls, for instance, were of white brick, the roof of green Eureka slates, and Portland stone facings were set off by a blue door and woodwork. But as so often with any project connected with Whistler, it aroused controversy. The original design made by Godwin for the house (Fig. 38), now in the Birnie Philip Bequest, Glasgow, seems simple and attractive enough, but it did not meet with the approval of the Metropolitan Board of Works and, before a licence was granted, this body insisted on several alterations which are by no means advantageous to the design; thus, as Godwin's final drawing reveals, decorative mouldings had to be placed on the plain surface. (Subsequently, too, various modifications were carried out by later owners.)

Some idea of how the interior looked during Whistler's brief occupancy of the house may be gained from the catalogue of the sale of the contents which was held on 18th September, 1879, after he had been adjudged bankrupt. This reveals that the dining room, the drawing room and breakfast room were laid with Indian matting; the studio had a Turkey carpet and the left front room a Persian carpet. The drawing room contained a butterfly cage on an ebonised stand with a stuffed bird in it, as well as two other butterfly cages with pulleys; and a pair of Chinese clogs, oddly enough, were also there. In the studio could be found a Japanese carved wood armchair, a Japanese carved wood bird-cage with painted panels and a small grindstone; his taste for Orientalism was confirmed by the thirty-nine Japanese hand screens in the dining room. All this makes curious reading today; but it suffices to suggest, however baldly, the atmosphere of the house where Whistler was to live for such a short time.

Connected with his preoccupations with decoration generally was his concern for the proper and harmonious presentation of his own works. Thus he designed special frames for his paintings in which, as in the *Purple and Rose: The Lange Lijzen of the Six Marks*, in the J. G. Johnson collection, Philadelphia, the predominant note of the picture—in this case the Oriental motifs—was carried on in its surround, so that the picture blended that much more effectively with a wall. A similar approach was followed by D. G. Rossetti and by Seurat, who, incidentally, was an admirer of Whistler's. Later, however, Whistler abandoned this sort of effect in favour of the familiar 'Whistler frame', which, as the

Pennells said,[1] was 'gold—green or red, not glaring—with reeded lines for his oils, watercolours and pastels; white, sometimes with purple or purple lines or patterns, for his etchings and lithographs'; and as his canvases were usually of a definite and similar size, a frame was invariably available for any one work.

Arising out of his solicitude for the individual presentation of each single piece was his desire to show his works publicly to their best advantage. In this, as in other respects, he was revolutionary. Instead of the usual cluttered impressions made at this period by one-man exhibitions of paintings, which were haphazardly arranged in a gallery, he felt that the gallery had to be made worthy of the exhibition; this view was implicit in his teaching. In 1874 for his first show at the Flemish Gallery, No. 48 Pall Mall, which contained thirteen pictures and fifty etchings, the walls were painted grey, and palms and flowers, blue pots and bronzes were introduced. The items were well spaced out, and for the occasion he designed the simple invitation card he later employed, on which the butterfly made its first appearance. As often, any innovation of Whistler's gave rise to trouble and he was engaged in a long and contentious correspondence with E. Clifton Griffiths, the owner of the Gallery, as to who should bear the cost for the decorations.[2]

It was also typical of Whistler's flair for decoration that he should have sailed under a symbolical banner—in his case, the Butterfly. He began to use this in the early 1870s and it was derived from the monogram of his initials, J M W or J A M W as they were before he dispensed with 'Abbott' from his name. At the start the letters are more or less recognisable, but, after some time, all connection with its origin disappeared. It was to appear as the signature to his letters, on his books, catalogues and pamphlets and, of course, his pictures. A sheet with butterfly studies, probably dating from about 1889, is at Glasgow University.

It is worth insisting on Whistler's achievement in the realm of interior decoration; it underlines his aim of securing a universal aesthetic and one which was revolutionary. It remains central to his ideas that the artist, although practising a variant on the 'art for art's sake' point of view, should adapt its principles to everyday life. There was fortunately a streak of practicability in his nature which induced him to favour a form of decoration which required no great expense and which suited the modern world. And this is one reason why his decorative principles are still relevant for a later generation.

[1] See also Pennell, I, p. 126.
[2] See *Whistler and his Circle: Letters and Documents*, published by L. Kashnor, Museum Street, London, 1927. Letters 26–31, 64–90. (Now in the Library of Congress, Washington.)

SEVEN

The Retreat to Venice

THE 1870s were an extraordinarily fertile period in Whistler's career; it was then that he found himself as an artist and that his considerable ambitions received effective expression. These are the years of the Nocturnes and of the portraits; and also of his experiments as a decorator, not to forget that in 1878 he made his first real trials as a lithographer, a medium admirably suited to render his evocative and mysterious style. Many of the prints he executed during this period were outstanding—those of Speke Hall (p. 75), of the Leyland girls and the splendid drypoint of the *Guitar Player* (Fig. 30); in the last his characteristic delicacy was complemented by strength. His etchings are also notable from another point of view: prints like *Adam and Eve, Old Chelsea, Old Battersea Bridge, Old Putney Bridge* and the remarkable *St James's* of 1878 (p. 90) show that he was finding his way towards the impressionistic style which blossomed out in the Venetian series.

Early in the 1870s Whistler also began drawing small sketches in charcoal. For these he used rough wrapping paper of many different tones, and variety was supplied by the application, on occasion, of touches of pastel. He tried his hand at various types of sketches: portraits, studies of models and hints for compositions. They are invariably delightful little sketches. He was after a graceful pose and his spontaneity and freshness of approach give them considerable personality. Many of them also stress his close connection with the classical ideal trend of the time. Yet as much as anything else, they opened the way for the splendid pastels done during his stay in Venice.

His work might be frequently attacked by hostile philistine critics, but this did not stop it from becoming widely known. He had ceased from showing at the Royal Academy after 1872 when his *Arrangement in Grey and Black: The Artist's Mother* (Fig. 28) was on view there, but his paintings and etchings appeared on exhibition on various occasions—at the Dudley Gallery (1872), the Flemish Gallery (June, 1874), and at the Grosvenor Gallery, the centre of the new aesthetic movement, in 1877, 1878 and 1879; moreover, a group of his etchings belonging to J. A. Rose was on view at the Liverpool Art Club in October, 1874.

In 1878 he also made nineteen drawings for use as illustrations in the catalogue of the 'Blue and White Nankin Porcelain' in the collection of the well-known surgeon, Sir Henry Thompson, which was shown by Murray Marks at his shop, 395 Oxford Street, London; this catalogue contained twenty-six plates in all and the remaining seven were drawn by Sir Henry Thompson himself. Eleven of Whistler's drawings are in the Art Gallery, Glasgow, and eight are in the Freer Gallery, Washington.

Whistler had now become something of a public personality, and to such an extent that a desire to put himself forward had taken a stronger hold of him. He

ST JAMES'S STREET
Etching, $10\frac{7}{8} \times 5\frac{7}{8}$ *in.* 1878. *British Museum, London.*

cut a figure in the artistic and fashionable world even if his relationship with Jo and later with Maud Franklin, his second *maîtresse en titre*, 'Mrs Whistler', as she was called, presumably rendered his position somewhat delicate in certain circles. It was understandable that he should have attracted attention; his art was revolutionary; his opinions outspoken; and his wit and charm undeniable. He dined out a great deal; thus in the 1870s, he told Mrs Leyland that he had 'dined with the great Bombay Parsee Arabs the Sassoons who are tremendous swells and whose old house and acres Leyland ought to have, as the estate is so large and so near London'.[1] He was also an excellent host in his own fashion, and the Sunday

[1] Undated letter (presumably 1876). Library of Congress, Washington.

breakfasts, which took place at noon, were novel affairs and well attended; they formed a sort of salon. He took great pains with the menu which he sometimes prepared himself, and the food was partly French, partly American. 'His buckwheat cakes are not yet forgotten', said the Pennells,[1] themselves American: 'He would make them himself, if the party were quite informal, and he never spoke again to one man who ventured to dislike them.'

The Pennells' words are revealing; they indicate the strong streak of aggression which activated Whistler's character and which was increasingly manifest whenever he was crossed. Thus he had pushed the unfortunate, and no doubt maddening, Seymour Haden through a plate glass window. He did not know when to stop and his treatment of Leyland was unpardonable; and his victim's letters to him at the time of the break-up, which are extremely pertinent, show how he appeared to a man who had been a friend and a sincere admirer. 'The fact is,' he wrote to Whistler,[2] 'your vanity has completely blinded you to all the usages of civilised life, and your swaggering self-assertion has made you an unbearable nuisance to everyone who comes in contact with you. There is one consideration, indeed, which should have led you to form a more modest estimate of yourself, and that is your total failure to produce any serious work for so many years.' This was very direct; but it was not really justified in respect of Whistler's artistic output.

Up to a point Whistler must not be judged by conventional standards and his disregard for many niceties of ordinary behaviour was an unfortunate part of his nature. It can be explained away, but hardly pardoned. And as his dealings with some of his associates prove, he was increasingly a victim of *hubris*, as for that matter was Wilde. His self-assurance was colossal; he seems to have gone under the illusion that everything would turn out all right in the end; indeed his courage in facing the financial difficulties which increasingly hemmed him in was amazing. He spent money recklessly, running up considerable bills with his unfortunate tradesmen. All this presumably stemmed from his conviction that the artist was a man apart, who did not require to bother about such matters. And he was not the man to compromise for the sake of money. 'It is better,' he once told Sidney Starr, 'to live on bread and cheese and paint beautiful things, than to live like Dives and paint pot-boilers.'[3]

But this situation could not continue indefinitely; in the end, the blow fell. It was sparked off by the libel case which he brought against Ruskin—one of the most celebrated cases of its sort in the history of the English courts. The remarks which the ageing and increasingly unstable critic had made about his picture, *The Falling Rocket* (Plate IV), were certainly offensive; his quip that he was 'flinging a pot of paint in the public's face', out of cockney impudence, was stupid and nasty. But for one who liked to exchange verbal attacks, Whistler showed a certain lack of

[1] Pennell, I, p. 190.   [2] Letter of 1877. Cited by Ferriday, op. cit., p. 413.
[3] Pennell, II, pp. 126–7.

humour; he might have been wiser to have let the whole affair drop. The case, which was held before Mr Justice Huddleston, makes fascinating reading, and, as might be expected, Whistler defended his position admirably, making use of the occasion to enunciate a brilliant explanation of his artistic principles. Although he won, with a farthing's damages, costs were awarded against him, and the expenses he incurred crippled him.

May of 1879 found him in the bankruptcy court, with the result that his collection of Blue and White as well as many of his pictures had to be auctioned at Sotheby's on 12th February, 1880. These misfortunes had a deleterious effect on his character; they heightened his bellicose streak and this side of his nature tended to come uppermost. The publication of *Whistler v. Ruskin: Art and Art Critic*, which took place six months or so before the final débâcle, was not only the first of his famous brown paper pamphlets; it was the announcement of a new approach. As transpires from a letter to Rose, his solicitor, he had felt that a principle was at stake: 'That is, the question at issue has really been not merely a personal difference between Mr Ruskin and myself, but a battle fought (by) the painters in which for the moment Whistler is the Quixote.'[1] Faced with a lack of understanding, conscious of the immense difficulties which greeted his attempt to secure the standard of perfection he desired and which so often eluded him, his rôle gradually changed. He started to take on less onerous tasks; his energy was increasingly reserved for the championship of his own cause and his intellectual and aesthetic position. He saw himself as the advocate of views, to him sound ones, which had been scorned. But momentarily he was compelled to vacate the field and withdraw to Venice—a project he had long nourished.

Whistler's fourteen months in Venice were hard ones and he had the misfortune to arrive when the city was undergoing her worst winter for thirty years. The former hero of the London dining table, the brilliant wit, was reduced to living in straitened circumstances, frequently being compelled to borrow small sums of money. But he had Maud with him and somehow or other they managed to survive; such was his natural resilience that he soon picked up. It was not long before he made his mark and Ralph Curtis has left a lively portrait of him at the time: 'Very late, on hot *sirocco* nights, long after the concert crowd had dispersed, one little knot of men might often be seen in the deserted Piazza San Marco, sipping refreshment in front of Florian's. You might be sure that was Whistler, in white duck, praising France, abusing England and thoroughly enjoying Italy.'[2]

Some amusing and revealing comments on Whistler's conduct in Venice were reported by Henry Woods, an English artist settled in the city, to Luke Fildes in London.[3] He wrote, in 1879: 'I could do with Whistler very well, but for his

[1] Undated, but received on 30th November, 1878. Library of Congress, Washington.
[2] Pennell, I, p. 273.
[3] L. V. Fildes, *A Victorian Painter* (*Luke Fildes*) (Issued for Private Circulation), 1962, pp. 51, 52, 58.

33 ARRANGEMENT IN BLACK AND WHITE:
THE YOUNG AMERICAN.
*Canvas, $75\frac{3}{4} \times 34\frac{3}{4}$ in. Butterfly signature.
First exhibited in 1878. Freer Gallery of Art,
Washington.*

34 HARMONY IN FLESH COLOUR AND
BLACK: MRS LOUISE JOPLING.
*Canvas, $75\frac{1}{4} \times 35$ in. Late 1870s. Birnie
Philip Bequest, University of Glasgow.*

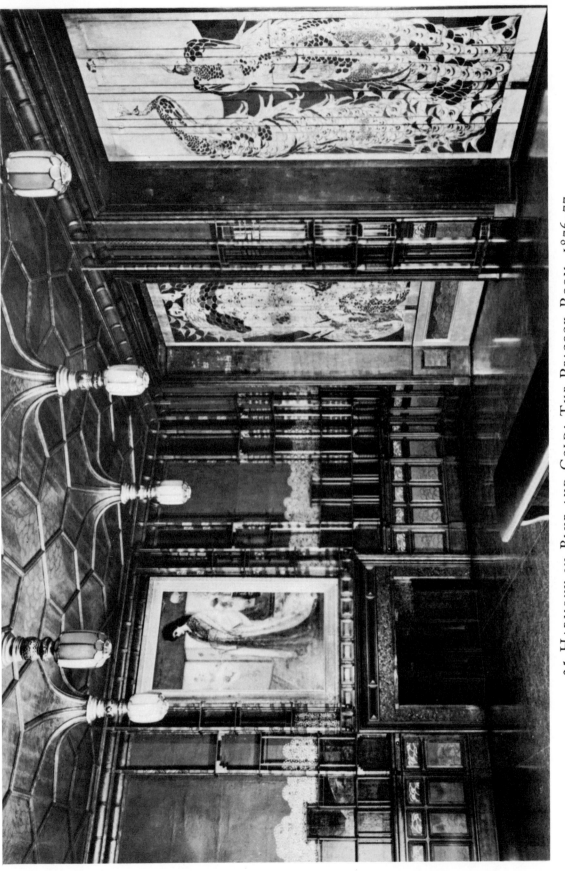

35 HARMONY IN BLUE AND GOLD: THE PEACOCK ROOM. 1876–77.
The picture on the wall is 'Rose and Silver: La Princesse du Pays de la Porcelaine'. Canvas, $78\frac{3}{4} \times 45\frac{3}{4}$ in.
The picture dates from 1863–64. Both the picture and the room are in the Freer Gallery of Art, Washington.

confounded conceit and ever-lasting seeking for notoriety. I cannot stand it. He has started two "moonlights" entirely from memory. They are, I must admit, remarkably true as far as they go. When I have time I will go to see him paint something; what I have seen of it here is so curious. His etchings will be very good I think.' Later he told his correspondent that 'Whistler is getting on very well with the etchings, but some little pastel drawings he has made are very excellent and interesting'. On his return to Venice after absence during the summer, Woods sent further news of Whistler to London: it was by no means flattering: 'Whistler, I hear, has been borrowing money from everybody, and from some who can ill afford to spare it. He shared a studio for five or six months with a young fellow named Jobbins. Jobbins never could work there with him in it. He (Whistler) invited people there as to his own place, and has never paid a penny of rent. He used all the colours he could lay his hands upon; he uses a large flat brush which he calls "Mathew," and this brush is the terror of about a dozen young Americans he is with now. Mathew takes up a whole tube of cobalt at a lick; of course the colour is somebody else's property. There are all sorts of conspiracies against Whistler. He is an epidemic, an old-man-of-the-sea. These young chaps were quite flattered at first when he joined them. It made me roar when I heard of his goings on amongst them, he evidently pays for nothing. There is no mistake that he is the cheekiest scoundrel out—a regular Ally Sloper. I am giving him a wide berth. It's really awful. There will be *Grande Festa* if he ever goes away.'

Yet the memory of him remained; Elizabeth Pennell recalled[1] how when she and her husband were there, four years after he had left the city, talk fell on him among the artists gathered at places like the Orientale café on the Riva.

His Venetian experiences were naturally highly important for determining the development of his art. He had the chance of broadening his aesthetic range, although his egotism never permitted him to forget his own work. Thus, after a visit to St Mark's, he said that the Peacock Room 'with the delicate harmony of its ceiling, was more splendid in effect than the Byzantine Church with its golden domes'.[2] Nevertheless, he made a careful study of certain Venetian painters, and he climbed upon a ladder to examine more closely the Tintorettos in the Scuola di San Rocco, expressing his delight at finding this master's technique similar to his own. It is difficult to know what he really meant by this remark. He voted Titian and Veronese 'great swells'[3] and Canaletto and Guardi were great masters. He also examined the Old Master drawings in the Accademia, a study that may have exerted some influence on his own sketches at this period.

During his Venetian days, Whistler painted exceedingly little, and a picture like that of a Gondolier which he started, remained unfinished as the model fell ill. Some pictures did not succeed; for the *Nocturne in Blue and Gold: St Mark's* (National

[1] *Nights*, 1916, p. 95.   [2] Pennell, I, p. 263.   [3] Pennell, I, p. 263.

Museum of Wales, Cardiff) remains unsubstantial and dark. On the other hand, the *Nocturne in Blue and Silver: The Lagoon, Venice* (Fig. 39), in the Museum of Fine Arts, Boston, is one of his most masterly canvases. The scene is almost ghostlike; the gondolas sneak through the night, with their own particular, almost insidious gliding movement, and the subtlety of the treatment—delicate tonal effects—is heightened by the faint tinges of green which occur in the picture; all is left to suggestion. In view of his liking for water and the appeal which Venice has for the artist, his failure to paint more while there is hard to explain; perhaps the very richness of the city put him off. Miss Edith Bronson, later the Countess Rucellai, who knew him then, said that he would always maintain that 'Venice was an impossible place to sit down and sketch in' as there was invariably 'something still better round the corner'.[1] Nevertheless, he did make a number of attractive watercolours, thus employing a medium which he does not seem to have used since his early days in Paris and which, from then onwards, he increasingly favoured; he also executed a considerable number of pastel sketches. Otto Bacher has described how he would search for motifs on foot or else float about in a gondola, laden with pastels.[2]

Pastel was a medium which suited him especially well; and it accorded with his mood at this time; moreover he was fortunate enough to find a store of coloured paper—brown, blue and pink—at an old warehouse just off the Merceria. The use of such paper gave him 'without any work at all, the foundation of a colour scheme which could be carried out in the simplest manner in the black chalk outline, and the few touches of pastel that completed the harmony'.[3] Moreover, the sympathetic colour of the paper allowed him to work straight away on it, and he did not 'ruin the surface and tire himself in getting the tone'. The pastels with their delicate and subtle accords of colour are not only adorable in themselves but significant works of art; they suggest that at this stage he realised, or sensed, that one of his main gifts lay in the notation of those vaporous transitory effects of atmosphere which occur in Venice and on the lagoons and which are almost Oriental in character.

Such surroundings offered simple, unaffected and uncomplicated subjects which, at this difficult pass, may have also brought to his mind memories of his early life in Paris; not that he was after the anecdotic detail as were many of the foreigners settled in Venice. Such notes revealed his marvellous sense of taste; he could work rapidly, seizing upon the characteristic qualities of a scene, and the labour, automatically ensuing when he faced up to a full-length portrait, was spared him. There was no need, on such occasions, to bother about his ambition, laudable but taxing, of becoming a rival to the great masters. Hence such works gain in spontaneity; nothing is forced about them. And the colouristic effects used could be strong: thus in the *Stormy Sunset*, in the Fogg Museum, Cambridge,

[1] Pennell, I, p. 263.   [2] Cf. O. H. Bacher, *With Whistler in Venice*, 1908.
[3] Pennell, I, p. 277.

pink, blue, green and yellow occur; in the *Alley in Venice* (Fig. 40), in the same institution, touches of pink appear on a brown and blue wall. His sheets are as exquisite in colour and as simple as the wings of a butterfly. And he emerged as a master of the intimate mood—as an artist who, in certain of his pictures, came close in spirit, though not in technique, to the French *intimistes*; his influence on Sickert was demonstrable and a number of this artist's small studies are clearly derived from Whistler's.

This was one side of Whistler's activity in Venice; his other main occupation was etching. He had arrived in Venice with a specific commission from the Fine Art Society to undertake a series of twelve etched plates of Venetian views. During his stay there, he produced some forty plates, of which a dozen appeared in *Venice, a Series of Twelve Etchings*, usually known as the 'First Venice Set', which was published by the Fine Art Society in 1880; and twenty-one came out in the group of twenty-six etchings published by Dowdeswell's six years later. These two sets establish Whistler's achievement as one of the most gifted etchers of the last century. The method he employed in doing them is made clear from his remarks to Mortimer Menpes: 'I began first of all by seizing upon the chief point of interest. Perhaps it might have been the extreme distance—the little palaces and the shipping beneath the bridge. If so, I would begin drawing that distance in elaborately, and then would expand from it, until I came to the bridge, which I would draw in one broad sweep. If by chance I did not see the whole of the bridge, I would not put it in. In this way the picture must necessarily be a perfect thing from start to finish. Even if one were to be arrested in the middle of it, it would still be a fine and complete picture.'[1]

These words make it obvious enough that Whistler worked direct from nature, putting down on the plate (and he would always carry a set about with him) the essence of the scene as he saw it. He did not care overmuch for topographical exactitude; he was mainly concerned to suggest the main outline of a scene and convey its atmosphere: in other words, his impression of it. In fact, certain prints are strongly reminiscent of French Impressionist painting. The small figures in his *Rialto*, for instance, recall those in Monet's *Boulevard des Capucines, Paris*, in the Marshall Field collection, New York, which was shown in the 1874 Impressionist exhibition; while an affinity of spirit can be sensed between the *Long Lagoon* and a picture like Renoir's *Vue de Venise* of 1881 (formerly with the Marlborough Fine Arts, London). It is not perhaps exaggerated to say that, as an etcher, Whistler gave more effective expression to the impressionist principles than some of the Impressionist *peintre-graveurs*. However, one should emphasise that the genesis of this approach is found in several of the etchings made in London during the late 1870s.

Although the plates were etched in Venice, only a few prints were actually printed in Venice, where he had the use only of a primitive old wooden press. The

[1] Op. cit., p. 22–3.

bulk were done in London. This is an important point as various revisions were undertaken to the prints while the artist was actually in the process of pulling them. The technique of the Venetian prints is superb and it is demonstrably clear, as that fine judge of graphic work, Campbell Dodgson, underlined,[1] that Whistler thought out for himself a new style of etching which would correspond to his interpretation

THE PALACES

Etching, $10\frac{5}{8} \times 14\frac{1}{8}$ in. One of 'The First Venice Set', 1880. Messrs. P. and D. Colnaghi, London.

of the special character of Venice. This was true not only of the etching but of the printing; for the exquisite rendering of atmospheric effect is achieved in the Venice plates by the over-varied inking of the plate with ink of paler or warmer brown, and the tone produced by the incomplete wiping away of the ink was something novel at that time and shocking to the orthodox. His ambition to secure tonal effects in his etchings matched the intentions he endeavoured to carry out in his paintings. And this technique was important for another reason; it was an indication of his attempt to produce a unique object in so far as practically every impression printed from the Venetian plates differed from another; thus he attempted to lessen

[1] *The Etchings of James McNeill Whistler*, 1922, p. 17.

the mechanical aspect of an art which is essentially reproductive. Another innovation due to Whistler, one by no means meeting with general approval, was his practice of 'trimming off the margins of each print, leaving only a small rectangle (or "tab") on which to put in pencil his famous "butterfly" signature. The signature was followed by the abbreviation *imp.* to show that he himself had printed and approved the impression.'[1]

At the present time, the etching, as an artistic medium, does not quite command the support it did thirty or forty years ago; our generation demands the stimulus of colour; but for those who delight in this branch of the arts, Whistler's etchings still exercise a potent fascination. There is so much to recommend them. The very lightness of touch for one thing is praiseworthy: this permitted him just to pick out the telling details in a scene, those which impart life to it. And he knew what to leave out so that the economy of treatment, like the brevity of wit, makes his point, as in that lyrical sheet *Bead Stringers*. To turn over a box of Whistler's Venetian etchings is to undertake a private and selective walk through the city; we may pause to enjoy the effect made by a gondola as it establishes its own pattern against the crumbling walls of a palace; we are introduced to some secret garden or provided with a view into a courtyard where, half-obscured by the darkness, strange faces peer out at us. These are figures which remind us of Ribot. With Whistler as our guide, we may set out in a gondola and gently glide along the canals, sharing in his enthusiasm for some ancient building, in which the façade glitters gemlike, and the doorway offers promise of the unknown. We are shown Venice, morning-cool, so that we see the far distance, almost mirage-like, and Oriental in its silhouette. Then, as night falls, this master technician, this virtuoso, so works his plate that he conjures up the play of moonlight (on such a night as this, we murmur perhaps) on a romantic palace and renders the crab-like appearance of a gondola nestling beside the wall. He makes us free of a secret, enchanted Venice; this is the Venice which Henry James evoked in his travel essays or in *The Aspern Papers*: a Venice where magic and mystery hold sway.

[1] H. Wright in introduction to *An Exhibition of Etchings, Dry-Points and Lithographs by Whistler* (Arts Council), 1954, p. 13.

EIGHT

The Siege of London

'WELL, you know, I was just home—nobody had seen me—and I drove up in a hansom. Nobody expected me. In one hand, I held my long cane; with the other, I led by a ribbon a beautiful little white Pomeranian dog—it too, had turned up suddenly. As I walked in, I spoke to no one, but putting up my glass, I looked at the prints on the wall. "Dear me! dear me!" I said, "still the same old sad work! Dear me!" And Haden was there, talking hard to Brown, and laying down the law—and as he said "Rembrandt", I said "Ha, ha," and he vanished and then—!'[1] With these characteristically vivacious, not to say aggressive, words Whistler announced his arrival in London. He was back—ready for the fray; and for the last twenty years of his life, he increasingly dominated the stage, winning a unique position in English art life, as a creative personality, as a self-appointed law-giver and as a controversialist.

The various exhibitions of his Venetian work held during the first three years after his return to London immediately aroused attention. The twelve Venetian etchings which form the first set were criticised in some quarters as being 'unfinished' when displayed at the Fine Art Society in December, 1880, but the group of fifty-three Venetian pastels, included in the same show, were highly successful and he netted 1,800 guineas from their sale. They certainly won the approval of Millais, who wrote to him that he was 'so *charmed* with your Venice work. . . . They gave me real pleasure. The gradations, tenderness and lovely tints of sunset, and sea quite delighted me.'[2] This provided yet another instance of the way in which Whistler's work was sympathetically received by his colleagues. Once again on this occasion he gave a practical turn to his belief that an artist's works ought to be gracefully shown in the appropriate setting, by hanging the pastels in a new and exciting manner and by decorating the exhibition gallery with an arrangement of gold and brown, which in his opinion was specially suitable for works in this medium. His friend Godwin has left a description of the gallery's appearance:

'First, a low skirting of yellow gold, then a high dado of dull yellow-green cloth, then a moulding of green gold, and then a frieze and ceiling of pale reddish

---

[1] Pennell, I, p. 269.   [2] Letter of 17th July, 1881, in Glasgow University.

brown. The frames are arranged on the line; but here and there one is placed over another. Most of the frames and mounts are of rich yellow gold, but a dozen out of the fifty-three are in green gold, dotted about with a view to decoration, and eminently successful in attaining it.'[1]

The second exhibition held in February, 1883, consisting of fifty-one etchings mostly of Venetian scenes, also received particular care and a sketch, formerly in the Howard Mansfield collection and now in the New British Museum, Connecticut, indicates the way in which he wished them to hang—with plenty of space between each print. This time white and yellow formed the dominant note; the wall was white with yellow hangings, the floor was covered with pale yellow matting and the couches with pale yellow serge; and the cane bottomed chairs were painted yellow. There were yellow flowers in yellow pots, and a white and yellow livery for the attendant. At the private view, the artist sported yellow socks just showing above his shoes and the assistants wore yellow neckties, while he distributed favours, 'wonderful little Butterflies', to his friends. Moreover, the Prince and Princess of Wales turned up for the occasion.

In all these manoeuvres, Whistler's skill as a public relations man was evident enough; more than ever he was 'news'. Doubtless his American blood sharpened his nose for publicity; and he dearly loved a battle. Thus he found a novel way of showing up the incomprehension of the critics who had gone for him and of stimulating controversy by printing in the catalogue of the 1883 exhibition extracts from some of the hostile and usually stupid observations made on his work: the half-title carried the neat remark—'Out of their mouths shall ye judge them'. Who can doubt that the compilation of this *sottisier* afforded considerable pleasure to the painter? And as a result of his stirring action many later art critics must have carried in their minds the image of another and equally skilful Whistler printing extracts from their writings and making them look foolish. The quotations provided are extraordinary, not least the comment of the *Glasgow Herald* that 'Whistler is eminently vulgar' as an artist; but the whole catalogue is a treasure store of such gobbets.

After the débâcle of the bankruptcy and the enforced retirement to Venice, Whistler had made a triumphant come-back with the public, at any rate, as far as concerned his etchings and pastels. But what of his other work? His ambitions were considerable and Alan Cole, who met him in May, 1881, reported that Whistler was 'taking a new studio in Tite Street where he is going to paint all the fashionables—views of crowds competing for sittings—carriages along the streets'.[2] Yet this is precisely the opposite of what happened, and the portraits

---

[1] In the *British Architect*, February, 1881, cited by Pennell, I, p. 292. For Camille Pissarro's comment on this exhibition and the charge that Whistler had stolen 'the idea of using yellow in the gallery' from him, see a letter to Lucien of 26th February: W. S. Meadmore, *Lucien Pissarro*, 1962, pp. 33–4.

[2] Pennell, I, p. 300.

he painted during the decade 1880–90, the years when he was such a London celebrity, show that his circle of patrons was restricted. He painted Lady Meux; in addition one or two other commissioned portraits came his way, but most of his sitters were friends or colleagues: Chase, Duret, Sickert, and Maud. In short, the fashionable world did not flock to him as it did to Boldini or Sargent, and until the very last years of his life, he could not be considered as a successful artist from the material point of view. Society's failure to make use of his services

" Who breaks a butterfly upon a wheel ? "

" His pictures form a dangerous precedent."—

VENICE.

"Another crop of Mr. Whistler's little jokes."
Truth.

1.—MURANO—GLASS FURNACE.

" Criticism is powerless here."—*Knowledge.*

2.—DOORWAY AND VINE.

" He must not attempt to palm off his deficiencies upon us as manifestations of power."—
Daily Telegraph.

3.—WHEELWRIGHT.

" Their charm depends not at all upon the technical qualities so striking in his earlier work."
St. James's Gazette.

A page from 'Etchings and Dry Points. Venice. Second Series'.

to a greater extent was sad; after all, one of his greatest gifts was a sense of *chic*. Nevertheless, in his portraits one senses the transition that was then occurring between Victorian and Edwardian England, one in which Society was tending to become both smarter and more cosmopolitan. Indeed, his portraits of Lady Meux could not have dated from the same period as those of Mrs Leyland or Mrs Huth.

In the first of the three portraits of Lady Meux—the 'state portrait' in the collection of Mr Ian Gilmour—she appears as a truly regal *grande dame* posed against a black background which emphasises the subtle contrasts between her

36 *Photograph of the stand at the Paris Exhibition of* 1878. *The cabinet and fireplace were designed by E. W. Godwin. The decorations, 'Harmony in Yellow and Gold,' are by Whistler.* 37 *Caricature by Max Beerbohm: 'Mr Whistler giving evidence in the case of Pennell v. the "Saturday Review" and Another'. Pen and wash.* $12\frac{3}{4} \times 10\frac{3}{4}$ *in.* 1926. *City Museum and Art Gallery, Birmingham.*

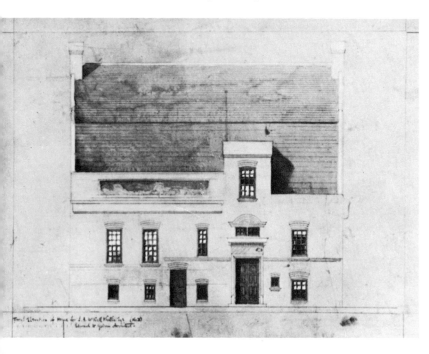

38 *Original front elevation of the White House, Chelsea, by E. W. Godwin. Pen and ink with wash.* $12\frac{1}{2} \times 17\frac{3}{4}$ *in. Birnie Philip Bequest, University of Glasgow.*

39 NOCTURNE IN BLUE AND SILVER:
THE LAGOON, VENICE.

Canvas, $20\frac{1}{8} \times 25\frac{7}{8}$ in. 1880. *Museum of Fine Arts, Boston.*

40 ALLEY IN VENICE.

Pastel, $10\frac{1}{4} \times 7$ in. 1880. *Fogg Art Museum, Cambridge, Mass.*

black velvet evening dress and her long cloak trimmed with white fur. The effects of silver on black again recall Whistler's love of Velasquez. His sense for delicate paint was revealed in his treatment of such accessories as the tiara, necklace and the bracelet on her gloved hand. The warmth and radiance of his sitter is conveyed in the picture; for instance, the modelling of her features and arms is firmer than in his other female portraits. His second portrait of her, the *Harmony in Flesh Colour and Pink* (Fig. 41), in the Frick collection, New York, was no less brilliant; this reveals a certain Titianesque influence and the pink and silver grey colours in her dress are attractively picked up in the drapery against which she is posed. The actual execution of this portrait is excellent; dashes of blue are found in the pink, while the edge of the drapery is rendered by means of broad dabs of paint. His skill is stressed by the way in which the passages of thicker pigment in the hat and dress give a certain stability to the composition; and it is painted on a coarse-grained canvas. Unfortunately, the third portrait of Lady Meux, representing her in furs and with a muff, was never finished; this painting which led to the break between them appears to have been destroyed.

Whistler's difficulty in finding patrons was understandable. Firstly, he was apt to prove cantankerous, and his row with Lady Meux was one example of this; secondly, he was too demanding; anxious to achieve perfection, he demanded what, to his sitters, must have seemed an excessive number of sittings. Many, in fact, are the stories (as already pointed out) which relate to his rubbings down and paintings out; the result is that few finished portraits exist on which to base a view of his style. Moreover, he demanded collaboration from a patron insofar as he, or she, had to be prepared to accept a pose by no means in accordance with the conventional ideas of the day. In this respect, a telling contrast can be made between his *Arrangement in Black: Lady in the Yellow Buskin: Lady Archibald Campbell* (Fig. 42), in the Philadelphia Museum, and Sargent's *Madame Gautreau*, in the Tate Gallery, which dates from 1882–4. Sargent's portrait, though extremely elegant and delightful, lacks the originality and painterly qualities found in Whistler's. He chose a most unusual stance, in which Lady Archibald is represented standing in left profile, with her head slightly turned towards the spectator; and the eye only reaches her face after having surmounted a short fur cape. Whistler achieves two distinct triumphs in the portrait; the theme is interpreted as a sort of still life in which the treatment of the hand holding the glove, which possibly owes something to Van Dyck, and the yellow buskin with its dash of grey paint, are examples of delicate tonal painting; and the charming, piquant and modish qualities of the sitter are finely caught. But it is noteworthy that, though Lady Archibald was sympathetic to the artist and herself interested in the modern movement, she was none too pleased by his portrait of her.

While painting Lady Archibald Campbell, Whistler was engaged on his *Arrangement in Flesh Colour and Black: Théodore Duret* (Fig. 44), in the Metro-

politan Museum, New York. Duret's description[1] of the way in which this picture
was painted shows that, having placed his sitter against a grey-rose coloured
material, Whistler started the portrait without any preliminary drawing, slightly
marking with chalk the place for the figure on the bare canvas and, at the end
of the first sitting, the scheme was there with the colours and tones it was to
possess in its definitive state. Then the artist's work began in real earnest and,
after the picture was almost brought to completion, it was rubbed out, begun
again and finally painted ten times; this over a long period. Duret realised that
what was involved was a question not so much of drawing as of colour and tone;
he understood Whistler's theory that to bring the whole picture into harmony
and then to preserve this harmony generally, the composition had to be totally
repainted if any repainting, in fact, was required. Whistler certainly managed to
achieve his aim in this picture—the sitter, as Duret pointed out, was meant to be
a gentleman returning home after a ball. Duret noted that the domino, in falling
to the left and covering part of the body, allowed the artist to do away with the
strict parallelity of the two sides of the body and thus to diversify its contours;
the rose tone which tinges the flesh, the fan and the domino 'is so managed that
the cold grey of the background seems to be flushed with rose'. When Duret
showed the portrait to visitors, the Pennells reported, he takes 'a sheet of paper,
cuts a hole in it, and places it against the background, to prove that the grey
when surrounded by white, is pure and cold, without a touch of rose, and that
Whistler got his effect by his knowledge of the relations of colours and his mastery
of the tones.'[2]

Whistler's love of the contrasts between black and white and his preoccupation
with tonal painting permitted him to succeed especially well when depicting a
figure in evening dress, and, in this respect, he lived up to Baudelaire's hope that
the 'true painter we are looking for, the one who can snatch its epic quality from
the life of today and can make us see and understand with brush and with pencil,
how great and poetic we are in our cravats and our patent leather boots'.[3] This
habit provided him with a means of securing the harmony he sought after, and,
significantly, in describing the deliberate artistic simplicity of Baron Charlus's
evening coat, Proust made a point of saying that it resembled a Whistlerian
harmony in black and white.[4]

Whistler's powers were excellently shown in the remarkable *Arrangement in
Black: Pablo de Sarasate* (Fig. 43), in the Carnegie Institute, Pittsburg, which
was finished by 1884; this is especially intriguing insofar as it gives the impression

[1] Op. cit., p. 101.   [2] Pennell, I, p. 308.

[3] Salon of 1845, in *The Mirror of Art: Critical Studies, by Charles Baudelaire*, ed. Jonathan Mayne,
1955, p. 38.

[4] In *Sodome et Gomorrhe*, Vol. II (i), pp. 33–4. See M. E. Cernowitz, *Proust and Painting*, 1945, p. 7
and passim.

that in some way the artist had identified himself with the sitter; and as T. R. Way and G. R. Dennis observed 'it curiously reminds one of Mr Whistler's own appearance when he stood upon the platform of Prince's Hall to deliver the "Ten o'Clock"[1] lecture'. He is every inch the virtuoso, proud, capable and temperamental, with his sensitively painted fingers holding his instrument with affectionate care. And the illusion is complete; we feel convinced that he is on the concert platform—an isolated figure seen from a distance, at a moment of hushed expectancy. The liveliness of the handling, the simplicity of the treatment and the elegance of the pose once again underline Whistler's debt to Velasquez; and in their account of this picture, Way and Dennis appropriately quote Whistler's remark that this master's portraits 'live within their frame and stand upon their legs'. This is precisely the achievement of this painting, and if the pen and ink sketch of the sitter reproduced by the Pennells was done prior to the portrait, it would suggest that the pose was captured at the start.

During the 1880s a change was noticeable in Whistler's portrait style. Some portraits are rather straightforward, like that of G. W. Lucas in the Walters Art Gallery, Baltimore, but others suggest a continuation of that concern for the inner life, the palpitating mystery of the personality which can be found in the *White Girl No. 4* (Fig. 18). This new spirit marks the *Green and Violet: Portrait of Mrs Walter Sickert* (Fig. 46: both in Fogg Museum, Cambridge), which was commissioned by her husband shortly after his marriage to her, at the same time as a portrait of himself, which is now lost. In the *Portrait of Mrs Sickert*, the actual brushwork has become broader and the paint flows more rapidly; this is indicated by such areas as the sofa and the dress. With great subtlety, the artist has provided a contrast between the dark passages of the dress and the rather indecisive, almost misty features—suggested rather than indicated—as if the artist was anxious to provide us with some glimpse of her changing moods. These effects of rather crumbly paint are also discernible in the sketch portrait of Sickert of about 1886 in the Municipal Gallery of Modern Art at Dublin. One should emphasise that both portraits are of friends, and, in the same way as Gainsborough felt more freedom when painting fellow members of the artistic world, so Whistler may have considered that he was entitled to enjoy a similar liberty with his circle.

Like any other painter who works on a number of different projects and with distinct aims in mind, Whistler was prepared to alter his technique to suit the subject chosen by him and indeed found it necessary to do so. The crisp properties of pigment had always appealed to him—as is seen from the *Six Projects*—but, at times, he was prepared to employ this rapidity of notation in portraits with a more realistic tinge. There is, for instance, a bravura quality about the bold *Une Jeune Fille des Rues* (belonging to Mrs J. Hampden Robb, Beverly Farms, Mass.) which, since it was presented to Duret before 1883, presumably

[1] *The Art of James McNeill Whistler, an Appreciation*, 1903.

dates from about this time. Although the title is in French and may have been due to Duret,[1] not Whistler, the girl was possibly one of the artist's Chelsea models, and, as such, it must be one of his first direct studies of this sort. The bolder handling may be due to the influence of Franz Hals, an artist he greatly admired; the style is reminiscent of that found in *The Chelsea Girl* (collection of the children of Mr and Mrs Potter Wear, Penllyn, Penn.), painted in about 1884–6, where the highly toned reds and the dash of yellow on the scarf certainly recall this painter.

The vivacity of his sketch technique was very noticeable during the 1880s. This is evident in a series of small oils of figures like the *Note in Flesh Colour and Grey: Dorothy Menpes* (collection: Michael Tree), painted prior to 1885, the *Note in Green and Brown: Orlando at Combe* (Birnie Philip Bequest, Glasgow), 1884, and the *Arrangement in Pink and Purple* (Cincinnati Art Museum) of 1881-5. These show that Whistler was experimenting in sharply accentuated dashes and dabs of colour and that in such works the provision of an overall tonality was not his main preoccupation; at times, as in the *Red and Pink: Little Mephisto*, in the Freer Gallery, Washington, shown at the Dowdeswell exhibition of 1884, the use of a rich pigment is combined with the more melodious harmonies of his general style. His variety during the 1880s was considerable; and the small, tender portrait *Arrangement in Grey: Master Samuel Manuel* (Fig. 48: Freer Gallery, Washington), with its Terborch-like quality, dates from this period; it was painted while he was friendly with Sickert.

In the catalogue of the first exhibition of his sketches held at Dowdeswell's in January-February, 1884, when the gallery was appropriately decorated with delicate rose on the walls, a white dado, white flowers in rose-flushed jars, while the Butterfly, tinted in rose, was on the invitation card, Whistler printed his 'Proposition No. 2', which declared that 'A picture is finished when all trace of the means used to bring about the end has disappeared' and 'the masterpiece should appear as a flower to the painter—perfect in its bud as in its bloom— with no reason to explain its presence—no mission to fulfil—a joy to the artist— a delusion to the philanthropist—a puzzle to the botanist—an accident of sentiment and alliteration to the literary man'.

His oil sketches, of which the high quality is sometimes overlooked, owing to their small size, are among his most attractive works—sensitive renderings of a particular moment in time, in which the emphasis is almost invariably, and happily, placed on delicate colour values, at times light, at others, dark in tonality. When he actually started to work in this vein—seascapes, townscapes, and landscapes—is not quite clear; however, his visit to St Ives in 1883–4 seems to have been decisive in turning him in this direction; from Cornwall he wrote to Paul Deschamps of the Society of French Artists that he was here 'doing a lot of curious

[1] This was given to Duret before 1883: see *Whistler Catalogue*, p. 64.

IV. NOCTURNE IN BLACK AND GOLD: THE FALLING ROCKET. Wood panel ($23\frac{3}{4}$ x $18\frac{3}{8}$ in.).
This was inspired by the fireworks displays in Cremorne Gardens, Chelsea, and dates from about
1874. This more than any other of Whistler's pictures provoked Ruskin's famous outburst
which led up to the Whistler-Ruskin lawsuit (The Detroit Institute of Arts).

little "games" '.[1] At St Ives was the sea, which appealed to him so strongly, and, as he wrote to Godwin: 'The country you know never lasts me long and if it had not been for the sea I should have been back before now.'[2]

He was there with Sickert, who had left the Slade School of Art in the previous year in order to help the older man with his etchings, and his influence may have proved helpful in developing this side of Whistler's art. He grew very close to the young artist and in an undated letter from this period, once declared that 'I have something quite lovely to show you—and you know I would rather you looked at my work than anybody else'.[3] Although, in later years, Sickert was critical of some of Whistler's work, the sketches, of which the majority are on panel, always won his approval. 'Whistler', he wrote, 'expressed the essence of his talent in his little panels—*pochades*, it is true, in measurement, but masterpieces of classic painting in importance. . . . The relation and keeping of the tone is marvellous in its severe restriction. It is this that is strong painting. No sign of effort, with immense result. He will give you in a space nine inches by four an angry sea, piled up, and running in, as no painter ever did before. The extraordinary beauty and truth of the relative colours, and the exquisite precision of the spaces, have compelled infinity and movement into an architectural formula of eternal beauty. Never was instrument better understood and more fully exploited than Whistler has understood and exploited oil paint in these panels. He has solved in them a problem that has hitherto seemed insoluble: to give a result of deliberateness to a work done in a few hours from Nature. It was the admirable preliminary order in his mind, the perfect peace at which his art was with itself, that enabled him to aim at and bring down quarry which, to anyone else, would have seemed intangible, and altogether elusive.'[4]

These words admirably sum up their qualities. The majority of these sketches, as he pointed out, were painted after Nature, and Whistler's eye for tone permitted him to capture the essence of a scene, whether a stretch of country, as in a *Note in Blue and Opal: The Sun Cloud* or a line of coast as in *Grey and Silver: The Angry Sea* (Fig. 50), or *Grey and Silver : The Life Boat* (all in the Freer Gallery); such works consist of no more than a few dashes of thick or thin paint; all that is required to provide the image of the essential qualities of the scene which the artist had observed in the course of his contemplation. The seascapes recall the sort of picture he had painted twenty years before on the Normandy coast when he was with Courbet. Nevertheless, in comparison with these, the treatment is more concentrated and selective; the dependence on his master has been shaken off and he has achieved a more personal expression. But these notes were not only devoted to the coast or the countryside; some of the most exquisite

---

[1] Letter of 8th January, 1884. Library of Congress, Washington.
[2] Letter of 30th January, 1884. Glasgow University.
[3] In the Library of Congress, Washington.   [4] Op. cit., pp. 18–19.

were of Chelsea, Paris or Dieppe. There is a touch of wit, epigrammatic in its brevity, about them, as if the artist had nonchalantly jotted down his sensations in front of a casual scene; and they form a natural sequence to the Venetian pastels. The sense of rhythmical paint which they contain is enticing; thus in the *Chelsea Shops* (Fig. 51), in the Freer Gallery, Washington, the slim moving figures seem to dance, as if to the sound of one of those barrel organs which are now, alas, a rarity in urban life: they almost look as if they were performing in a ballet.

Failures and vicissitudes certainly occurred in the latter part of Whistler's life—and these have been allowed to dominate the view of him and his work to the exclusion of these small late oil studies. They remain an essential and highly attractive part of his contribution. They are extraordinarily pure, like the pastels of Boudin and the sketches of Degas, with whom they share some affinities. They recall, too, some of Corot's early works—those grey-toned sketches in which a passing mood in Nature is swiftly and effectively captured. And one suspects that Whistler looked at Corot; like him, he managed to secure the right tone. With these, rather than with his more formal paintings, his claim that painting and music are related is best illustrated; and we may be moved by them in rather the same way as we are by an *étude* by Chopin or Schumann, heard from a window, or by a line from Mallarmé or Verlaine which haunts the memory. There is something very tantalising about such pictures; several possess a curious and pervasive mystery. The evident delight in the construction of patterns made up of lines and shapes (which echo Vermeer and have a relationship to Vuillard) constitute part, a large part even, of their appeal; but, at times, we are conscious of a certain almost enigmatic content, as in a painting by Odilon Redon. The two old women who appear in *Gold and Orange: The Neighbors*, in the Freer Gallery, Washington, are at first sight no more than casual figures who have caught his eye: they recall the 'popular types' he sketched in Venice. Yet they are something more beside: theirs is almost a mocking air, as if they were present to hint at experiences which the artist did not quite care to reveal.

One aspect of these oil studies or notes is particularly intriguing—the titles borne by some of them. The majority are no more than titles which render into words the effects seen by the artist in Nature and which he was attempting to reproduce in paint. However others, like the *Angry Sea* or the *Sad Sea*, suggest that the artist was using his vision of Nature in order to render a mood, either his own or one which, at a specific moment of time, he perceived in Nature. Whistler's distaste for moralistic or anecdotic subject matter needs no emphasis, but his refusal to accept this sort of content did not mean that he banished all content from his work, and his pictures may include emotional reverie. It is here that the Japanese influence may again have been partly responsible for the form taken by his work. Japanese art, as we have seen, helped him to formulate his vision of a painting as an arrangement or harmony. One wonders if, at the same time, his absorption in the Japanese aesthetic consciously, or unconsciously, and as a conse-quence of the intensity of his absorption, led him to reach a position not all that dissimilar from that of Ezra Pound and the Imagists. In looking at these studies, one gains an impression rather akin to that received when reading a typical Imagist poem or a Japanese *haiku*, from which much Imagist poetry derives. According to Pound, in a poem of this type one image superposes itself upon another: so with a picture like *Red and Pink: La Petite Mephisto* (Freer Gallery, Washington), we think firstly in terms of the colours—red and pink—and then as we take in the subject, *La Petite Mephisto*, we grasp that the content has been fixed by the exactness of the tonalities.

The broad range of his style in the 1880s is made clear in the three extraordinary watercolours of Dutch scenes in the Freer Gallery, Washington, which date from his visit to that country in 1884; in a work like the *Grand Canal, Amsterdam*, the grey and yellow toned paint enabled him to achieve an exquisite translucence and convey a sense of mystery, while the red light from a window, reflected in the water, conjures up a sonorous note.

The studies may be said to reflect the private side to Whistler's life. And their existence would hardly be suspected from the public persona so triumphantly and even blatantly offered to inspection. During the 1880s, he blossomed out into a highly social figure. He lived first at 13 Tite Street, which he decorated in yellow, so that it gave the impression, as Howell said,[1] that one was standing inside an egg. Later, he moved to a studio in the Fulham Road, which was painted white throughout and with a touch of yellow in the rugs and matting. His financial situation had sufficiently improved for him to start collecting again—Blue and White, which stood on the table, and eighteenth-century silver, of which he was extremely fond. And he could entertain. His parties were well attended and J. E. Blanche, who lunched with him in June, 1882, gave a vivid description[2] of the company present on this occasion, with its 'Lords and Ladies', as well as a few Americans. Whistler was always an original host, and for this luncheon, which was a buffet affair, the guests could help themselves to smoked fish, pressed beef, *poulet en pâte à la crême*, polenta, *oeufs au safran*, *kari de langouste*, raw peas, steamed potatoes, moselle cup and coffee. Whistler presided, brilliant, witty, ever in command of the situation.

It was no wonder that, at this time, Whistler was the foil to Wilde and that the two men engaged in a series of spirited exchanges. Wilde for a time became a close friend of his, and the decoration of his house, and his poetry, were influenced by the Whistlerian approach. They certainly had much in common, although the painter was never the writer's intellectual equal; fundamentally, their aims were

[1] Pennell, I, p. 300.
[2] A long and fascinating account of this lunch occurs in a letter to his mother (19th June, 1882). See *La Pêche aux Souvenirs*, 1949, p. 145.

different. This opposition between their views was brought to a head in Wilde's review of the 'Ten o'Clock' in *The Pall Mall Gazette*; in this he maintained that the artist is 'the resultant of a certain *milieu* and a certain entourage, and can no more be born of a nation that is devoid of any sense of beauty, than a fig can grow from a thorn, or a rose blossom from a thistle'.[1] Moreover, Wilde had a warmth which was not really present in Whistler's character; and that they fell out was perhaps inevitable; their letters to one another throw light on the personalities of each.

A change came over Whistler's life when he met Beatrix (Trixie)—the wife of E. W. Godwin. The daughter of John Birnie Philip, the sculptor, she had married Godwin in 1876 and 'was a lively young lady given to hero-worship, Bohemian, and an amateur in several arts'.[2] Her life with Godwin, who was unfaithful to her, was not especially happy, and she came to be on close terms with Whistler, who gave her lessons. By all accounts Godwin was content that his friend should look after her; nevertheless, his death must have proved a relief to them both, and there is a ghoulish story—very much in the Maupassant manner—of Whistler, Mrs Godwin and Lady Archibald Campbell eating their lunch off the top of poor Godwin's coffin as an open farm waggon carried his remains to the graveyard.

Whistler himself was not altogether free when he met Trixie as he was living with Maud; it was only after several sharp encounters between the two women (on one occasion poor Maud burst a blood vessel) that Trixie carried the day. His portrait, *Harmony in Red: Lamplight* (Fig. 52), at Glasgow, painted in 1886, is radiant with happiness and Trixie's good sense and warmness are admirably conveyed. Lady Milner, who remembered the artist and Trixie calling on her mother before their marriage, described how the pair were beaming: 'He, well over fifty, was in love like a boy, so that we all four sat and beamed together. Their devotion to each other lasted until her death and he never got over her death.'[3] She evidently knew how to manage him and to moderate his outbursts: this was apparently recognised by his friends as Sickert wrote to her asking her to prevail upon Whistler not 'to be drawn by Menpes's rot'.[4] On this occasion, which related to an interview given by Menpes to *The Pall Mall Gazette* on interior decoration, her intervention does not seem to have been of any use. However, Mrs Whistler sometimes got her way; when her husband painted Mrs Sickert's eyes brown when, in fact, they were blue, she herself changed them to the correct colour.[5]

In the same year as his marriage, Whistler became President of the Society of

[1] 21st February, 1885.
[2] D. Harbron, op. cit., p. 118.
[3] *My Picture Gallery, 1886–1901*, 1951, p. 5.
[4] Sickert to Whistler, letter of December, 1888—January 1889. Glasgow University.
[5] H. M. Swanwick, *I Have been Young*, 1935, p. 131.

41 HARMONY IN FLESH COLOUR AND PINK:
LADY MEUX.
Canvas, 75¾ × 36½ in. *Butterfly
signature. First exhibited in* 1882.
Frick Collection, New York.

42 ARRANGEMENT IN BLACK:
LADY IN THE YELLOW BUSKIN:
LADY ARCHIBALD CAMPBELL.
Canvas, 84 × 43 in. *First exhibited in*
1884. *Museum of Art, Philadelphia.*

43 ARRANGEMENT IN BLACK:
PABLO DE SARASATE.
*Canvas, 85½ × 44 in. Butterfly
signature. 1884. Carnegie Institute,
Pittsburgh, Penn.*

44 ARRANGEMENT IN FLESH COLOUR
AND BLACK: THEODORE DURET.
*Canvas, 76⅛ × 35¾ in. Butterfly
signature. First exhibited in 1885.
Metropolitan Museum of Art, New York.*

British Artists, to which he had been elected a member in 1884. As nearly always with his concerns, matters did not go smoothly. It was typical of his enthusiasm and energy that he should have thrown himself into the task of reorganising this body, and soon after he had joined it, Claude Phillips, that shrewd critic, perceptively declared: 'The eccentric Mr Whistler has gone to a neglected little gallery, the British Artists, which he will probably bring into fashion.'[1] His flair was evident in practical as well as in artistic matters and, after sending Queen Victoria an illuminated address on the Society's behalf, on the occasion of the Jubilee, and executing a series of twelve etchings, accomplished in one day, of the Naval Review, it was hardly surprising that the Society received a Royal Charter, and became the Royal Society of British Artists. Naturally, Whistler was high-handed; but it was not in his nature for him to take any other line.

He believed in quality and took his task seriously; thus he wanted to exclude those works which seemed to him to be not up to standard and to decorate the rooms in an appropriate fashion. He tried to practise his idea of artistic hanging and decoration—for a visit of the Prince of Wales he painted the doors and dados yellow and designed a velarium (p. 110) to ensure better light—but his innovations, which a few years later were to be followed by the Secession groups in Germany and Austria, led to controversy. The inevitable happened: Whistler and a minority resigned in 1888 and as he said in a famous *bon mot*—'the Artists have come out and the British remain'.[2] The difference between his point of view and that of the bulk of the members was contained in his successor's, Wyke Bayliss's words: 'Whistler's purpose was to make the British Artists a small, esoteric set, mine was to make it a great guild of the working artists of this country.'[3] As Whistler himself declared: 'I wanted to make the British Artists an art centre, they wanted to remain a shop.' It was characteristic of his staunch belief in the importance of being earnest—about art—that principle won.

His relations with the New English Art Club were also beset with difficulties. This society, the most *avant garde* of its kind in England, had been founded in 1886 and largely consisted of Paris trained students who were critical of the Royal Academy. At first the sympathisers with the Club or the members of it included various painters belonging to the Newlyn School or the Glasgow School. However, by 1889 power had come into the hands of the 'impressionists', a clique headed by Sickert which included Brown, Paul Maitland, Steer, Sidney Starr, and Théodore Roussel. Whistler was never an active member of the Club although he did send a picture and an etching to the 1888 exhibition and a pastel to the 1889 exhibition. On this occasion he was elected by the votes of the exhibitors, to the jury. However, he fell out with the Club in 1894 over the Eden affair, when he felt, not without some justification, that his fellow painters had let him down. Despite all this, several members of the Club, like Sickert, Starr and Roussel,

[1] Pennell, II, p. 58.   [2] Pennell, II, p. 71.   [3] Pennell, II, p. 73.

were close followers of his style, and homage to him and an echo of his doctrine are found in the preface which Sickert[1] wrote for the exhibition of 'The London Impressionists,' a ginger group from the New English Art Club, which held a show at the Goupil Gallery in 1889, the same year in which Sickert organised an exhibition of Whistler's works in the College for Working Men and Women, Queen's Square, London. It was a pity that Whistler could not have overcome his prickly egotism in order to become the leader of these young men who owed so much to his example. But he was always the lone wolf.

[1] Sickert's preface is reprinted in D. S. MacColl, *Life Work and Setting of Philip Wilson Steer*, 1945, pp. 175–6.

The Society of British Artists Exhibition. Pen and ink, 7 ×6 in. About 1886. Ashmolean Museum. Oxford.

NINE

The Ten o'Clock

ALTHOUGH priding himself on the creation of a new style, Whistler was no iconoclast. Since those early days when he had copied Boucher, Ingres, Velasquez and Veronese in the Louvre, he had been a frequenter of museums and his affection for Oriental art and Greek terracottas was considerable. He was always a close student of the Old Masters, and though the range of his taste was narrow, one only wishes that he had written the 'Conversations in the National Gallery' with which he had once toyed; how brilliant and provocative it could have been. In general, he was more interested in painting from the seventeenth century onwards, but he was not blind to the achievements of earlier schools. The Italian painters of the fourteenth and fifteen centuries mainly seem to have appealed to him from a technical point of view, and he told Eddy that 'The Old Masters used simple pigments which they ground themselves. I try to use what they used. After all, it is not so much what one uses as the way it is used'.[1]

He was not quite at ease with Michelangelo and Raphael and his comments on these masters reveal much of his own temperament. 'Michelangelo,' he said,[2] 'was 'a tremendous fellow, yes; the frescoes in the Sistine Chapel?—interesting as pictures, but with all the legs and arms of the figures sprawling everywhere, I could not see the decoration. There can be no decoration without repose: a tremendous fellow, but not so much in the David and other things I was shown in Rome and Florence, as in that one unfinished picture at the National Gallery. There is often elegance in the *loggie* of Raphael, but the big frescoes of the *stanze* did not interest me.' On the other hand, he admired Tintoretto, whose technique, in his view, resembled his own, and Titian: this artist's *Man with a Glove* in the Louvre was one of his favourite pictures. Caravaggio appealed to him too; so did Hogarth and Canaletto and he maintained that the last was the equal of Velasquez and Guardi. His views could prove startling. Poor Menpes must have been surprised when one day in the National Gallery, Whistler, after carefully examining a Rembrandt portrait, exclaimed: 'It's gummy! It has a gummy, what you call a fat, juicy quality about it that I don't like.' He added 'these so-called master-

[1] *Recollections and Impressions of James A. McNeill Whistler*, 1903, p. 73.
[2] Pennell, II, p. 209.

pieces are not great works. They are pictures that you look at and are interested in merely because of their technical dexterity.'

On the other hand, the portraits of Frans Hals and, of course, the Dutch cabinet painters captivated him; he would happily fasten on a Terborch, but such was his perfectionism that he would perhaps find only one small face in it which appealed to him. 'Ah,' he would say, 'what have we here? Rembrandt has never painted anything to equal this little bit of flesh. Here we have no trick of the brush, no dexterity, no obviously marvellous technique; but the little lips, and the eyes, and the pearly tones of the shadows, all seem a part of the flesh tone, just as they are in nature; and it is so utterly simple that one is quite unaware of any apparent clever-ness.' He would hardly look at the rest of the picture, muttering to himself, so Menpes recorded: 'He's got it this time but he does not understand blacks'.[1]

Is it surprising that Whistler made people sit up? Undoubtedly he was often playing to the gallery with his remarks and attempting to shock; perhaps this was the case when he sneered at Constable. 'What an athletic gentleman he must have been! And how enamoured he evidently was with his palette knife! Many a happy day, I warrant, Constable spent with that palette knife, and then—Oh dear! the country—how wearied one must get of green trees!'[2] Here he is comparing Turner to Claude: 'Well, you know, you have only to look. Claude is the artist who knows there is no painting the sun itself, and so he chooses the moment after the sun has set, or has hid behind a cloud, and its light fills the sky, and that light he suggests as no other painter ever could. But Turner must paint nothing less than the sun—and he sticks on a blob of paint—let us be thankful that it isn't a red wafer as in some of his other pictures—and there isn't any illusion whatever, and the Englishman lifts up his head in ecstatic conceit with the English painter, who alone has dared to do what no artist would ever be fool enough to attempt! And look at the architecture: Claude could draw a classical building as it is; Turner must invent, imagine architecture as no architect could design it, and no builder could set it up.'[3]

His opinions about modern painting were also eccentric in some ways. Obviously in the early years he was taken by Courbet and Bonvin, as well as by his friend Fantin-Latour, but he was guarded about many of his celebrated contemporaries, especially the Impressionists: he was even downright critical: and he disliked Cézanne. He considered Frith the equal of Manet and he admired J. C. Hook and Sir William Orchardson! He also liked the most unexpected artists and J. E. Blanche noted[4] that the weekly drawings which Grévin contributed to the *Journal Amusant* appealed to the witty side of his nature and that he derived some inspiration from them. Nevertheless, Whistler was not a complete 'reactionary' and as President of the International Society, and as the energetic promoter of their two

[1] Menpes, op. cit., pp. 79–80.   [2] Op. cit., pp. 81–2.   [3] Pennell, II, p. 178.
[4] *La Renaissance Latine*, 15th June, 1905, pp. 353–78.

45 ARRANGEMENT IN
BLACK NO. 3: SIR
HENRY IRVING, IN
THE CHARACTER OF
PHILIP II OF SPAIN
IN TENNYSON'S
'QUEEN MARY'.

*Canvas, $84\frac{3}{4} \times 42\frac{3}{4}$ in.
1876–85. Metropolitan
Museum of Art,
New York.*

47 MISS MAUD FRANKLIN.
Canvas, 24½ × 16 in. Fogg Museum of Art,
Cambridge, Mass.

46 GREEN AND VIOLET: MRS WALTER SICKERT.
Canvas, 34 × 24 in. Butterfly signature. First exhibited in 1894.
Fogg Museum of Art, Cambridge, Mass.

famous exhibitions in London, he made space available for many of the foreign *avant-garde*. After all, a painter finds in the work of other men only what he wants to see and what serves his own ends; and Whistler was essentially self-centred; yet his remarks, if they sometimes seem rather outrageous, at least have the merit of being refreshing and stimulating.

His considered aesthetic views were expressed in the famous 'Ten o'Clock' Lecture, which he delivered at the Prince's Hall before a select group of fashionable and intellectual society in February 1885. Among those present were Godwin, Moore, Sickert and Wilde, who was seated next to Herkomer! 'The scene,' as Wilde said,[1] 'was in every way delightful; he stood there, a miniature Mephistopheles mocking the majority! He was like a brilliant surgeon lecturing to a class composed of subjects destined ultimately for dissection, and solemnly assuring them how valuable to science their maladies were, and how absolutely uninteresting the slightest symptoms of health on their part should be.' Although W. C. Alexander once told the Pennells that, for him, there was nothing particularly new in the lecture, since it summed up what the artist had often said, it did provide an effective means for presenting his ideas to a wider audience, especially as the lecture was repeated at Oxford and Cambridge, at the Grosvenor Gallery, London, and even in the house of the Cobdens at Dieppe where the young Daniel Halévy heard it.

It was typical of Whistler's character and especially of his self-confidence that he sought to embody his doctrine in words, and his attitude is underlined in his many letters to the press. These had given him some experience with writing, and already he had tried out his hand at composition in the pamphlets on the Ruskin case, *The Piker Papers*, which dealt with his quarrel with the Painter-Etchers Society, and the *Paddon Papers: the Owl and the Cabinet*, which also treated of controversial matters. He took immense care with his literary efforts; the draft of the 'Ten o'Clock', among the Whistler papers at Glasgow, reveals something of a Flaubertian ambition to secure the *mot juste*.

Characteristically when giving his lecture Whistler explained that he was appearing in the rôle of 'The Preacher'. He argued that although art was much spoke about and was 'upon the Town', as he phrased it, and that people were 'told how much they shall love Art, and live with it', any conception which saw art in this manner was wrong; art had nothing to do with bettering other people.

'She is, withal, selfishly occupied with her own perfection only—having no desire to teach—seeking and finding the beautiful in all conditions and in all times, as did her high priest, Rembrandt, when he saw picturesque grandeur and noble dignity in the Jews' quarter of Amsterdam, and lamented not that its inhabitants were not Greeks.

[1]*The Pall Mall Gazette*, 21st February, 1885. For the exchange between Wilde and Whistler, see *The Letters of Oscar Wilde*, ed. Rupert Hart-Davis, 1962, pp. 170–1.

'As did Tintoret and Paul Veronese, among the Venetians, while not halting to change the brocaded silks for the classic draperies of Athens.

'As did, at the court of Philip, Velasquez, whose Infantas, clad in inaesthetic hoops, are, as works of Art, of the same quality as the Elgin marbles.'

Whistler then disposed of the conception that earlier epochs were particularly conducive to the arts—notably ancient Greece and fifteenth-century Italy and 'that we, of to-day, in gross contrast to this Arcadian purity, call for the ungainly, and obtain the ugly'. Whereas, he explained, at the start most men went out hunting or to battle, there was 'found among them one . . . who took no joys in the ways of his brethren . . . this designer of quaint patterns . . . this deviser of the beautiful—who perceived in Nature about him curious curvings, as faces are seen in the fire—this dreamer apart, was the first artist.' As Whistler saw it, the artist 'went beyond the slovenly suggestion of Nature, and the first vase was born, in beautiful proportion'. In his view, the excellence of art and architecture in Greece or until modern times, was due to the fact that the artist alone was responsible for design, 'so that all peoples continued to use what *the artist alone produced*'. His argument is not precisely clear as to when or how the change took place but he claimed that 'the world was flooded with all that was beautiful' until there arose a new class, who discovered the cheap, and foresaw fortune in the facture of the sham.' Apparently he correlated the 'tawdry, the common, the gewgaw' with the Industrial Revolution and 'the people—this time—had much to say in the matter—and all were satisfied. And Birmingham and Manchester arose in their might—and Art was relegated to the curiosity shop'.

Taking up his point that the artist had to go beyond 'the slovenly suggestion of Nature', Whistler then enunciated his famous dictum that: 'Nature contains the elements, in colour and form, of all pictures, as the keyboard contains the notes of all music. But the artist is born to pick and choose, and group with science, these elements, that the result may be beautiful—as the musician gathers his notes, and forms his chords, until he bring forth from chaos glorious harmony.

'To say to the painter, that Nature is to be taken as she is, is to say to the player, that he may sit on the piano.

'That Nature is always right, is an assertion, artistically, as untrue, as it is one whose truth is universally taken for granted.'

It was the rôle of the artist to create on the basis of what he found in Nature and, as he pointed out, in one of the most provocative, as it is one of the most attractive, passages in the Lecture: 'And when the evening mist clothes the riverside with poetry, as with a veil, and the poor buildings lose themselves in the dim sky, and the tall chimneys become campanili, and the warehouses are palaces in the night, and the whole city hangs in the heavens, and fairy-land is before us—then the wayfarer hastens home; the working man and the cultured one, the wise man and the one of pleasure, cease to understand, as they have ceased to see, and Nature, who, for once, has sung in tune, sings her exquisite song to the artist alone, her son and her master—her son in that he loves her, her master in that he knows her.

'To him her secrets are unfolded, to him her lessons have become gradually clear. He looks at her flower, not with the enlarging lens, that he may gather facts for the botanist, but with the light of the one who sees in her choice selection of brilliant tones and delicate tints, suggestions of future harmonies.

'He does not confine himself to purposeless copying, without thought, each blade of grass, as commended by the inconsequent, but, in the long curve of the narrow leaf, corrected by the straight tall stem, he learns how grace is wedded to dignity, how strength enhances sweetness, that elegance shall be the result.'

Whistler was ever forthright. In rapid succession he disposed of the various types of men who write about art: and, on this score, his words are as relevant now as then. He went on to make the point: 'Art had become foolishly confounded with education—that all should be equally qualified.' There was no reason, he argued with sound sense, why everyone should appreciate art: 'Art happens—no hovel is safe from it, no Prince may depend upon it, the vastest intelligence cannot bring it about, and puny efforts to make it universal end in quaint comedy, and coarse farce.'

The claim is sometimes made that Whistler was only concerned with an aesthete's point of view; this is surely disposed of by his criticisms, doubtless well founded, of dilettantism: 'The voice of the aesthete is heard in the land, and catastrophe is upon us.' With some smart asides at contemporary fashions, Whistler claimed for the artist a status as a full-blooded creative force: 'The artist, in fullness of heart and head, is glad, and laughs aloud, and is happy in his strength, and is merry at the pompous pretension—the solemn silliness that surrounds him.

'For Art and Joy go together, with bold openness, and high head, and ready hand—fearing naught, and dreading no exposure.'

Nor did Whistler look back nostalgically to the past; he flatly rejected any idea that his own age was a backward one, firmly maintaining that: 'It is false, this teaching of decay'.

His refusal to acknowledge a concept of decadence stemmed from his conviction that art flourished independently of the *Zeitgeist:* his was an anti-materialist position; so he claimed that the means at the artist's disposal were the same as those in the past: 'Colours are not more since the heavy hangings of night were first drawn aside, and the loveliness of night revealed.'

He also shot down the argument that a link exists between 'the grandeur of Art and the glories and virtues of the State'. Art, in fact, can be found 'among the opium-eaters of Nankin'. Visualising art as a cruel jade, he finds that one of her lovers was the master of Madrid (i.e. Velasquez) who towers above all others. 'So in all time does this superb one cast about for the man worthy of her love—and Art seeks the Artist alone. Where he is, there she appears, and remains with him—

loving and fruitful—turning never aside in moments of hope deferred—of insult—
and of ribald misunderstanding; and when he dies she sadly takes her flight,
though loitering yet in the land, from fond association, but refusing to be consoled.'

Refusing to concede that we must give up hope, he closed with the exhortation
that: 'We have then but to wait—until with the mark of the Gods upon him—
there come among us again the chosen—who shall continue what has gone before.
Satisfied that, even were he never to appear, the story of the beautiful is already
complete—hewn in the marbles of the Parthenon—and broidered, with the birds,
upon the fan of Hokusai—at the foot of Fusi-yama.'

Whistler was a painter, not a philosopher; consequently we must not expect from
him logical and tightly reasoned arguments. While correctly reproving those held
by the 'vice of subject', he did not perceive his own inconsistency in arguing that
more value was to be found in painting twilight than the sunshine which makes the
artist turn aside 'to shut his eyes'. He was affirming his own point of view—one
that did not allow for the existence of an alternative taste.

His ideas were by no means as novel as he liked to believe. The plea that art was
superior to nature had already been ventilated in France by Baudelaire in 1846
and the devotion to art as an activity independent of life had been championed by
Gautier; in England, the ideal of 'art for art's sake' was held and expressed
with great subtlety by Walter Pater. He was the heir to a tradition which also
embraced the idealistic tradition of aesthetics as formulated by Kant and Hegel;
moreover, points of contact occur between his theory and those of Shelley, Keats
and Newman; thus in Whistler, Mr Williams has suggested,[1] the Romantic trap
has been sprung. Although today Whistler's lecture may sound a little thin and
even pretentious, within the context of the era its meaning is much more positive:
as an affirmation that the artist was not required to concern himself with subject
matter but with lines and colours—with the presentation of an abstract image
based on a study of Nature. Above all, it was a triumphant statement that the artist
did not need to consult the past; his subject matter could stem from contact with
the contemporary world. If one thinks of the generally rather grim state of English
painting at this era, his words assume their true significance—and his own practice
both reveals and confirms the excellent use to which he put his precepts.

The publication of his lecture had various consequences. It brought about a
rupture with his old friend Swinburne, who wrote a critical review of it in the
Fortnightly Review.[2] In his reply[3] to this, Whistler was less than fair in his handling
of Swinburne's strictures, excising those passages in which the poet, by giving his
adversary some praise, might seem to weaken the painter's own sense of mis-
judgement and disdain. Thus he suppressed sentences like the following: 'Much
that Mr Whistler has to say about the primary requisites and the radical conditions

[1] *Culture and Society, 1780–1950*, 1961, p. 173.   [2] Vol. xliii (January-June, 1888), pp. 745–751.
[3] See *The Gentle Art of Making Enemies*, pp. 250–8.

49 L'echarpe Rose.
Panel, 10 × 7 in. *Birnie Philip Bequest, University of Glasgow.*

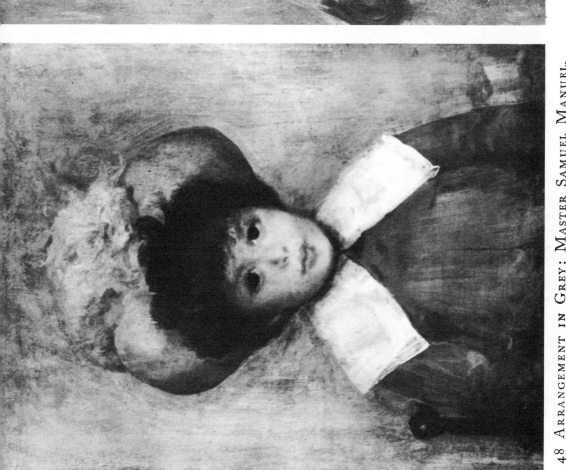

48 Arrangement in Grey: Master Samuel Manuel.
Canvas, 20 × 15 in. Early 1880s. *Freer Gallery of Art, Washington.*

50 GREY AND SILVER: THE ANGRY SEA.
Panel, $4\frac{5}{8} \times 8\frac{1}{4}$ in. First exhibited in 1884. Freer Gallery of Art, Washington.

51 CHELSEA SHOPS.
Panel, $5\frac{1}{4} \times 9\frac{1}{4}$ in. 1880s. Freer Gallery of Art, Washington.

of art is not merely sound and solid good sense as well as vivid and pointed rhetoric, it is a message very specially needed by the present generation of students in art or letters.' Another was: 'Some of these passages or phrases are very jewels of epigram or of illustration.' And he dropped Swinburne's conclusion: 'But if we must more or less respectfully decline to accept "The Preacher" as a prophet, we may all agree in applause of the brilliant humour which barbs the shafts of good sense and sound reasoning aimed by the satirist at the common enmities of all work—"a teeming, seething, busy mass, where virtue was industry, and where industry was vice".'

Although Whistler's lecture occasioned the loss of an old friend, it did permit him to make a new one—Mallarmé.[1] The two men already knew each other casually and had various common aquaintances like Manet and Duret, who was one of the painter's warmest defenders in France. But it was Monet who actually brought the two men together; he invited Mallarmé to lunch at the Café de la Paix in Paris in order to meet Whistler, 'who would be happy to get to know you better'. This occasion led to further encounters between poet and painter. One result of their friendship was that Mallarmé, assisted by Vielé-Griffin, undertook the translation of the 'Ten o'Clock' into French and this duly appeared in the Revue Indepéndante in May, 1888, and later as a separate publication.

For once all went smoothly; and no acid correspondence took place. On the contrary, Whistler sent Mallarmé a note telling him that he was touched with 'the sympathy shown in every line for my work, and which inspires you as, with un-parallelled success you find in your admirable prose, the form, in my view the ideal one, for rendering the "Ten o'Clock" into French'.[2] Mallarmé, for his part, was no less courteous, informing him that he had found the last corrections all the more easy to make as 'I sympathise entirely with your artistic vision'.[3] There was nothing forced about their exchange; the two men were truly fond of each other as may be grasped from the evident sympathy which informs Whistler's perceptive lithograph of the poet (p. 120), with its flickering intensity, and Mallarmé's concentrated and precise prose portrait of the painter, of which the following is an extract: *Un Monsieur rare, prince en quelque chose, artiste décidément, désigne que c'est lui, Whistler, d'ensemble comme il peint toute la personne—stature, petite à qui la veut voir ainsi, hautaine, égalant la tête tourmentée, savante, jolie; et rentre dans l'obsession de ses toiles.*[4]

The entire portrait with its intuitive understanding of the real Whistler, of his passion, of his '*vital sarcasme*', and of his desire for perfection, is a miracle of delicate yet in no way sycophantic compliment. Mallarmé's poetry certainly pleased

[1] See Carl P. Barber, 'Whistler and Mallarmé' in the *College Courant* (Glasgow), xiii (1960), pp. 14–19. See also Henri Mondor, *Vie de Mallarmé*, 1941, passim.
[2] See Barber, op. cit., p. 15. [3] See Barber, op. cit., p. 16.
[4] In *Médallions et Portraits* (Pléaide edition), 1945, p. 531.

Whistler and his response to the dedication of the *Billet à Whistler* was grateful. 'You ought to know, *mon cher ami*', he wrote, [1]'that I was enchanted in reading the delightful sonnet.

> *. . . la rue*
> *Sujette au noir vol de chapeaux.*

Splendid. Everybody is thrilled and we are all very proud—especially myself

> *. . . puisse l'air*
> *De sa jupe éventer Whistler.*

That is really superb and very dandyish at the same time.'

The two men, so different in character yet so alike in their love for the exquisite, felt at ease in one another's company; Whistler became one of the privileged group, who attended the legendary evenings, the famous *Mardis* in the rue de Rome, where his presence was obviously appreciated.[2] Here he could find that convinced belief in the value of art, in the value of art as an absolute necessity, which he had missed in England. Both Whistler and Mallarmé were exceedingly scrupulous artists who devoted an exacting attention to their art: one expression of their perfectionism was that both should have favoured an individual *mise en page* for their writings. Their ambition was to capture the nuances which they, and only they (so they felt), could perceive in the changing world around them; obviously as a man of letters, Mallarmé went further in his concern to find the verbal equivalents for the intricacies of his mind; and his thought, as rendered in words, was more concentrated, hermetic and subtle than the painter's. To try and make out any real case for the direct influence of the one upon the other would prove a little foolish, perhaps. Yet it is not exaggerated, I hope, to suggest that certain affinities may be detected in their mutual desire to discover the precise phrase or tonality (as the case may be) which would convey, as far as colours or words can convey, the almost inexpressible quality of their sensations. These resemblances must not be pressed too far; they are no more than hints—intimations. Thus with a line like—

> *Que dore le matin chaste de l'Infini*

the arrangement of words seems to conjure up before one's eyes one of Whistler's small panels in which a tender shaft of light touches in the outline of the horizon— itself an indication of the infinite. The affinities between the two men are further brought out when one remembers the attention each gave to technical means so

---

[1] Letter of 19th November, 1890. See *Mallarmé* (Pléaide edition), pp. 1426–7 (translated from French).

[2] See Henri Mondor, *Vie de Mallarmé*, 1941, passim. In particular quotations from G. Rodenbach in *L'Elite*, 1899, and E. Bonniot in 'Les Mardis de Mallarmé' in *Marges*, 1936 (Mondor, pp. 526-654).

designed that one would provide tonal interplays of colour, and the other alliteration and assonance. In phrases like—

> *Je veux que mes cheveux qui ne sont pas des fleurs*
> > *(Hérodiade)*
>
> *Mais, chez qui du rêve se dore*
> *Tristement dort une mandore*
> > *(Une dentelle s'abolit)*
>
> *sans mâts, sans mâts*
> > *(Brise Marine)*

the rhythmic repetition of words and sounds achieve a harmony which emphasise, and that much more delicately, the content of the verse; meaning is nourished by the repetition of words; with Whistler's art an analogous effect is secured by tonal painting and variations of colour within a set *gamme*.

Moreover, in the Sonnet—

> *Dame*
> > *sans trop d'ardeur à la fois enflammant*
> > *La rose qui cruelle ou déchirée et lasse*
> > *Même du blanc habit de pourpre le délace*
> > *Pour ouïr dans sa chair pleurer le diamant*
>
> > *Oui sans ses crises de rosée et gentiment*
> > *Ni brise quoique, avec, le ciel orageux passe*
> > *Jalouse d'apporter je ne sais quel espace*
> > *Au simple jour le jour très vrai du sentiment,*
>
> > *Ne te semble-t-il pas, disons, que chaque année*
> > *Dont sur ton front renaît la grâce spontanée*
> > *Suffise selon quelque apparence et pour moi*
>
> > *Comme un éventail frais dans la chambre s'étonne*
> > *A raviver du peu qu'il faut ici d'émoi*
> > *Toute notre native amitié monotone.*

the image conjured up by means of *rose, blanc, pourpre* presents an experience comparable (in its own manner) to that afforded by the *Symphony in Flesh Colour and Pink: Mrs Leyland* (Fig. 32) in the Frick Gallery, New York, or the *Harmony in Flesh Colour and Pink: Lady Meux* (Fig. 41), also in the Frick Gallery.

Finally, another common bond linked them; a single-minded, almost slavish prosecution of their aims—this arose from their realisation of the almost imponderable and impenetrable difficulty of suggesting the substance of their intentions and of providing a statement of its essence in a form which took into account its different facets. Both felt that it was incumbent upon the artist to conjure up in his work something of the inexpressible mystery of Nature; both realised that the means at their disposal fell short of their ambitions; and, as Professor Schmidt[1] has stated in respect of Mallarmé, 'the poem is both the instrument of the metaphysical vision of the poet and the limitation of this vision'. This is perhaps also the case with Whistler, and his cutting words about Nature and his boast that the artist improved on Nature, could be interpreted as being a recognition, nonetheless, of her mocking character; that she was his rival as well as his inspiration.

[1] *La Littérature Symboliste*, edition of 1947, p. 11.

Whistler's lithograph portrait of Mallarmé for the frontispiece of the first collected edition of 'Vers et Prose', 1893.

❧ T E N ❧

The Turn of the Tide

BY the 1880s Whistler had won an international reputation and his work was shown in Austria, France, Germany, and the United States. As a leading member of the *avant garde*, he was invited, for instance, to contribute to the first show held by the very progressive Society of Les XX in Brussels, and he was represented in their group exhibitions of 1886 and 1888. It was typical of his fastidious concern for the way in which his work should be hung that he forwarded a plan for its arrangement to Octave Maus.[1] Although one critic considered his pictures in the first exhibition to be *assez désillusionnant*,[2] his painting exerted a considerable influence in Brussels, then a major centre of the Symbolist movement; and sympathy for his art is especially apparent in the paintings of Finch and Van Rysselberghe and possibly in certain seascapes by Ensor.

In France, too, he was staging what might almost be called a come-back. He sent two pictures to the 1885 Salon and in May and June, 1887, fifty small oils, water colours and pastels were included in the International exhibition held at the Galerie Georges Petit in Paris, in which Monet, Morisot, Pissarro, Renoir, Rodin and Sisley were represented. His admission to this exhibition, so Monet told Duret,[3] had been voted for with acclamation; and Monet had apparently been deputed by his friends to pass on the invitation to the artist. His work, though with some reserve, was appreciated by many of the leading French painters, and in 1883 Camille Pissarro spoke well of his etchings: 'They are splendid, correctly drawn, strong.'[4] But this painter's judgment was more measured about his oils and, after the 1887 Paris show, he told his son: 'Whistler has some very fine bits of sketch in paint, forty-two. He was honoured with the best places, he also has a large portrait of a lady, the painting is completely black. Nor is their

---

[1] See *Trente Années de Lutte pour l'Art*, 1926, p. 25.   [2] Op. cit., p. 25.

[3] Letter of 6th March, 1887, once in the possession of MM. Loliée, Paris. In March, 1887, Monet wrote to Georges Petit, the art dealer, that he could count on Rodin, Whistler, Renoir and himself for an exhibition (MS. sold, Hôtel Drouot, 26th February, 1853, Lot 80). On 13th May, 1887, Monet wrote to Paul Durand-Ruel that: 'Whistler est aussi des nôtres avec de très jolies choses'; see *Les Archives de l'Impressionisme*, ed. L. Venturi, 2 vols., 1939. Vol. II, p. 326.

[4] *Letters to Lucien Pissarro*, ed. John Rewald, 1943, p. 27.

any luminosity either. Whistler, by the way, does not care for luminosity. His little sketches show fine draughtsmanship. In the corridor he has some very good, in fact quite superior etchings, they are even luminous, which is strange for an artist who does not aim at this in his colour.'[1] Pissarro correctly discerned the difference evident between Whistler's style in the two separate media.

This was an appropriate moment for his art to win admirers in France. Thus in his review of the Salon of 1889,[2] Felix Fénéon drew attention to the *action de M Whistler*; this was precious owing to the fact that it operated on artists who were intelligent and did not abdicate their personality. In 1891 the French Government, as the result of pressure by Mallarmé, Duret and Roger-Marx, bought the *Arrangement in Grey and Black No. 1: The Artist's Mother* (Fig. 28), for the Luxembourg Museum for 4,000 francs. This acquisition aroused considerable excitement in French artistic circles, and the picture's influence may be clearly seen in several of Toulouse-Lautrec's portraits,[3] notably that of G. H. Manuel, which dates from the same year. Moreover, Seurat sympathised with Whistler's ideas on nocturnal painting[4] and his own view that art was a harmony coincided with Whistler's, not that the latter explicitly stated that colours possessed an emotive sense in the way advocated by Seurat. Although a reaction was later to occur against Whistler's painting in France, the critical writings of Gustave Geffroy and Charles Morice, not to mention the many passages in Proust's novel, *A la recherche du temps perdu*, about his work, emphasise the extent to which he was admired in that country. Proust met him once and treasured a glove the artist left behind. At the close of the century, he was considered as 'a psychologist and as an artist who evoked the soul' and as a 'sort of Mallarmé of painting, a visionary to be classed amongst Poe and Maeterlinck, a necromancer shut up in his ivory tower, in the middle of a garden with dark poppies in which the icy atmosphere is never warmed by the sun'.[5] A special vocabulary was needed to describe his work; such was the opinion of Morice, who considered that this should contain

---

[1] Op. cit., p. 108.

[2] In *La Cravache*, 29th June, 1889, reprinted in *Oeuvres*. Introduction by Jean Paulhan, 1948, p. 175.

[3] Cf. M. Joyant, *Henri de Toulouse-Lautrec*, 2 vols., 1926, Vol. I, p. 122.

[4] Kahn mentions Whistler saying in the *Ten o'Clock Lecture* that the painter's art begins especially when artificial lights are lit: 'Seurat et moi en parlâmes, un jour d'été torride, dans ce petit atelier du Boulevard de Clichy . . .; Seurat me dit: "C'est un propos de grand peintre. Whistler a raison." ' Cited in *Les Dessins de Georges Seurat*, 1928. Mr Robert L. Herbert has kindly told me that the same author in 'Chronique: Les peintres étrangers à L'Exposition' in *La Vogue*, iv (3rd September, 1889), p. 233, declared that: 'La peinture de M. Whistler possède en France un adhérent, M. Blanche; ses théories sur l' art, en dehors de toute technique et même en dehors de la théorie des arrangements de lignes et des correspondances de couleur, en possèdent un autre: M. Seurat,' Mr R. H. Wilenski has suggested that Whistler's *Portrait of his Mother* might have inspired the right background of Seurat's well known pictures, *Les Poseuses*. See *Seurat*, 1951, p. 2.

[5] J. E. Blanche, op. cit., pp. 353-78.

words like *fluide, effluve, spiritisme, fantastique, supre-terrestre, supra-sensible, extra-lucide, abstraction plastique, rayonnement physique*.[1]

The 1880s and 1890s were, in fact, a period when the Symbolist movement was in the ascendant in France. Various points of contact, for instance, may be discovered between Whistler's ideas and those of Gauguin, who also affirmed his belief in the connections between music and painting, and between his technique and that of Carrière. As Whistler had partly derived his own inspiration from the French 'art for art's sake' doctrine, it was natural that he should have drawn close to the aesthetic symbolists. The theorist of the idealist group, André Mellerio, had explained[2] that Nature provided a far-away point of departure for painting; everything really rested in the cerebral and entirely subjective transformation which occurred in the artist's hands. Thus the artist was not concerned with sensation alone—the statement of something perceived independently of the will—but with the idea which we extract from it; it is this and this alone, which the artist seeks to express without worrying overmuch about the exact objective facts which were its origin. Whistler himself never went the whole way in creating a language of independent symbols—such a route was barred to him owing to the foundation of his style upon the observation of Nature. Nevertheless, his portraits do attempt to provide an idea of the essence of a personality while his mere studies, the notes, offer something in the nature of an abstracted image of the external world.

In England, his fame was growing no less rapidly, and in 1891 the Corporation of Glasgow, as a result of a petition by a group of members of the Glasgow School, purchased the *Arrangement in Grey and Black No. 2: Thomas Carlyle* (Plate V) for 1,000 gns. He was now one of the most notable painters of the day; as the Pennells rightly said 'it was the Turn of the Tide'. The exhibition of his 'Nocturnes, Marines and Chevalet Pieces' at the Goupil Gallery in March, 1892, was something of a triumph. It had been arranged by the artist with the dealer David Croal Thomson, a genuine lover of painting and the author of a book on the Barbizon school. Whistler's many letters to this dealer, now in the Library of Congress, Washington, reveal the thoroughness he devoted to the preparation of the exhibition—and the labour was by no means wasted; as Croal Thomson declared: 'Crowds thronged the galleries all day, and it is quite impossible to describe the excitement produced. I do not know how it fared with the artist and his wife during the day, but about five o'clock in the evening Mr and Mrs Whistler came in, though they would not enter the exhibition; they remained in a curtained off portion of the Gallery near the entrance. One or two of their most intimate friends were informed by me of the presence of the painter, and a small

[1] *Quelque Maîtres Modernes*, 1914, pp. 24–5. However, Maurice Denis pointed out that by 1905 Whistler had a bad press and that his influence was at an end. See *Théories 1890–1910*, 1913, p. 194.

[2] *Le Mouvement Idéaliste en Peinture*, 1896.

reception was held, for a little while, but, of course, by that time the battle was over and won, and there were only congratulations to be rendered to the master.'[1] The catalogue contained a selection of past criticism; this must have made galling reading now that Whistler had won success.

The market for his pictures had certainly improved and when Alexander Reid, the Glasgow art dealer, acquired the *Princesse du Pays de la Porcelaine* (Freer Gallery, Washington), Mrs Whistler, at her husband's behest, wrote[2] to him saying that he should ask 2,000 gns. for it and try and sell it to the Potter Palmers of Chicago, then staying at Brown's Hotel in London. A year later, in fact, he told Way that only 'now I fancy I see fortune looming on the horizon!— and I might really be rich! who knows!'[3] Indeed, a year later he disposed of his *Harmony in Blue and Gold: The Little Blue Girl* and three pastels and water-colours to his munificent patron C. L. Freer, for no less than 13,000 gns.![4]

At this time he was also concerned with examining and even repainting some of his earlier pictures, and in a revealing letter[5] written from Paris in 1892 to Richards of Berners Street, London, he took him to task for not removing the varnish from the 'large Nocturne of Cremorne' as he wanted to 'paint upon it'. The same letter contains some interesting information about his method: 'The little Thames picture and the seapiece are painted, as well as I remember, in one go and consequently are not so much impasted.'

His fame had been further spread by the publication, in June of the previous year, of *The Gentle Art of Making Enemies*. Its appearance had been heralded by the trouble that often cropped up where Whistler was concerned. The idea for such a book had been originally suggested to the artist by Sheridan Ford, but, after having given him permission to gather material, Whistler changed his mind, deciding to bring out the volume himself. Sheridan Ford, however, went ahead with his project, printing it in Belgium; and much time and energy was spent by the artist in securing its suppression. This fascinating and famous volume was a sort of collected edition of his earlier writings—the letters to the press (which seem to have been prompted by his disagreement with an article on his work in the *Saturday Review* for 1st June, 1867), the Ruskin case exchanges, the 'Ten o'Clock', the controversy with Swinburne—and, as such, it makes entertaining reading.

Today, however, it must be admitted that some of the squibs seem a trifle damp and the wit rather too contrived. Yet in general it does give the impression of an extraordinary lighthearted and whimsical spirit; that this is so is also due to

---

[1] Pennell, II, pp. 120–121.
[2] Letter to A. Reid, 30th May, 1892. Freer Gallery, Washington.
[3] Letter of 7th December, 1893. Freer Gallery, Washington.
[4] Letter to C. L. Freer, 1894. Freer Gallery, Washington.
[5] 12th June. 32 Rue de Tournon. Library of Congress, Washington.

52 HARMONY IN RED: LAMPLIGHT:
MRS WHISTLER.

*Canvas, 74¾ × 35 in. Butterfly signature.
First exhibited in 1886. Birnie Philip Bequest,
University of Glasgow.*

53 ETHEL PHILIP READING.

*Panel, 8⅜ × 5 in. 1894. (The sitter married
Charles Whibley in 1895). Birnie Philip
Bequest, University of Glasgow.*

54 PURPLE AND GOLD: PHRYNE THE
SUPERB: BUILDER OF TEMPLES.

*Canvas, 9¼ × 5⅜ in. Butterfly signature.
First exhibited in 1901. Freer Gallery of Art,
Washington.*

55 GREY AND SILVER: LA PETITE
SOURIS.

*Canvas, 23 × 15 in. Butterfly signature.
First exhibited in 1898. Birnie Philip Bequest
University of Glasgow.*

the choice of type and presentation. Max Beerbohm may sound a little high-falutin but there is much in what he writes: 'Such a book I treat tenderly, as one would a flower. And such a book is, in its own brown-papered boards, whereon gleam little gilt italics and a little gilt butterfly, Whistler's *Gentle Art of Making Enemies*. It happens to be also a book which I have read and read again. . . . Yet it comes as fresh as when first . . . it came into my possession. A flower freshly plucked, one would say—a brown and yellow flower, with a little gilt butterfly fluttering over it. And its inner petals, its delicately proportioned pages, are as white and undishevelled as though they never had been opened.'[1]

The feeling for style that is such an integral part of Whistler's character comes out in his writings; on the whole, he went in for short sentences and, on occasion, especially in the 'Ten o'Clock', he employed a biblical sounding language which properly accorded with his rôle as the Preacher. His turn of phrase could be singularly effective; and he certainly spent much time polishing his prose. The note struck in his writings was essentially conversational; they are often the expressions of an immediate reaction (albeit sharpened so carefully) either to an idea or to a person. Their aim was usually to plant a barb neatly and effectively in the flank of an opponent. Whistler had a natural gift for repartee; this was made evident in the exchanges which took place between him and Ruskin's barrister at the famous trial. His writing, therefore, at times rings with the sharpness of such cut-and-thrust dialogue. Not that he always came off best; the shrill note can prove a trifle too insistent and his logic was by no means faultless. However, the elegance of his writings and witticisms continue to please and they reflect his serious belief in his art—not to forget himself.

Naturally, Whistler devoted considerable attention to the typography of his writings; and he was responsible for the choice of the type, the spacing of the text, the *mise-en-page* and the use of butterflies. He introduced into his typography, as Holbrook Jackson explained,[2] a conversational lightness; its outstanding characteristic is an impression of decoration but without the use of ornament or illustration—except for the Butterfly. In all his printing, Whistler used an original style; this is apparent in the brown paper covers employed for his exhibition catalogues and his printed works. Mr Jackson also observed that his typography did not rely on any special (or expensive) aids; he took what lay to hand. His *mise-en-page*, so elegant and lively, was doubtless derived from the layout used in his letters. Thus, in this department as in others, he achieved the harmony he desired; and one which, in this case, was composed of printing, paper, and binding.

In the last twenty years of his life, Whistler devoted much of his time and energy to graphic work, producing no fewer than two hundred and thirty prints, of which the majority were etchings. Most of these were small impressionistic notations of

[1] *Yet Again*, 1909, pp. 104–5.   [2] *The Printing of Books*, 1938, pp. 88–98.

London or Paris street life; as such, they may be seen in relation to the small panels which also date from this period. He was never without his set of plates and his trips to Belgium (1887) and Touraine (1888) resulted in a number of delightful etchings, in which he showed his appreciation of architecture, and small narrow streets. However, not all his prints were on a modest scale; for instance, his visit to Amsterdam in 1889 seemed to have given him a special stimulus; he etched seventeen plates, all of which are exceedingly rare owing to the fact that they were never published, and in these he returned to what Harold Wright once called his 'grand manner'. He was inspired by the combination of old houses and water (an echo of the Venetian years?) as in the *Square House, Amsterdam* or the *Embroidered Curtain*. Some connoisseurs have even maintained that one print from this series, the *Zaandam*, put him in a class with Rembrandt. His business sense was emphasised in the letter[1] he sent to Huish of the Fine Art Society offering him the rights on the Dutch series of etchings.

Lithography also engaged his attention, and his enthusiasm for this medium may have been due to Mrs Whistler's liking for it. He certainly showed himself to be a versatile and varied lithographer, making a number of rather elegant and sweet prints like the *Steps, Luxembourg Gardens* and *The Pantheon, from the Terrace of the Luxembourg Gardens* (both of 1894) and 'conversation pieces' like *The Sisters* and *Confidences in the Garden*, which might have served as illustrations for a story by Henry James or Edith Wharton.

The attraction lithography held for Whistler is not always recognised, but his interest in it is underlined in his many letters to Thomas Way, his printer. His conscientiousness in this medium is brought out in one of these letters, in which, interestingly enough, the artist was prepared to acknowledge that he could fail. In this he declared: 'Here is another drawing—and really this time, unless the paper plays us very false, we ought to get rather a pretty result—for the work is simplicity itself—most direct—and with no fumbling and retouching.

'It ought to be of the brightness of the Rue du Furstenberg—which by the way seems to be a favourite—and it is on the new paper—better in quality we will hope than the other. Make it give all that it will.

'We will call the drawing "La fruitière de la rue de Grenelle".

'Do write me a line to say it has arrived safely, and telling me how it looks on the stone—If it comes off as well as the Rue Furstenberg we will be happy.

'My notion was, as I told you, that in the case of the little forge, the failure was very much owing to my work—which had lost part of its freshness—and was too fatigued. This time it ought to come off better.'[2]

In addition he made five coloured lithographs of which the *Yellow House, Lannion* (1893) with its yellow, green, brown and black grey tones was the most

---

[1] 3rd September, 1889 (from Hotel Brack, Doelen). Library of Congress, Washington.
[2] Undated letter. Library of Congress, Washington.

successful. These experiments indicated that he had kept abreast of the spirit of the time, which set much store on lithography. Although the daring simplifications of colour and line associated with such pioneers as Toulouse-Lautrec and Bonnard never occur in his prints, he was certainly aware of their work and his studio remains contained various volumes of the illustrated series of *L'Estampe Nouvelle*, the Austrian *Vers Sacrum* publication, as well as several prints by Toulouse-Lautrec.

The success of the 1892 exhibition at Dowdeswell's had aroused considerable

RUE FURSTENBERG, PARIS
*Lithograph, $8\frac{3}{4} \times 6\frac{3}{8}$ in. Early 1890s.
Messrs. P. and D. Colnaghi, London.*

interest in his potentialities as a portrait-painter and one consequence was that the Duke of Marlborough commissioned him to paint his portrait; but although he made a drawing of him, now at Glasgow, the Duke's death prevented its completion. The later portraits give some signs of strain and of his almost desperate efforts to achieve what he wanted. This was made clear when he painted the *Arrangement in Black and Gold: Comte Robert de Montesquieu* of 1891, in the Frick collection, New York. The sitter was one of the most elegant and bizarre dandies of the time, and a possible model for Des Esseintes in Huysman's novel *A Rebours*; he was on friendly terms with the painter to whom he addressed a quantity of letters, now at Glasgow University, and to whom in part payment of the portrait he presented the French bedstead given to Madame de Montesquieu, the governess of the young King of Rome, by Napoleon; this is now in the Victoria and Albert Museum, London. Montesquieu sat to Whistler seventeen times during his month's stay in London in 1891, and, as reported by Edmond de Goncourt: 'The preliminary sketch, with Whistler, is apparently a mad rush at the canvas, one or two hours of feverish frenzy, from which the thing emerges all wrapped up in its covering. Then there are long, long sittings during which, most of the time, the painter brings his brush up to the canvas, does not touch it, throws the brush away, and takes another—with the result that in three hours he will add about fifty touches to the painting, each touch, in his words, removing one veil from the sketch's covering. Sittings in which it seemed to Montesquieu that Whistler, with his fixed attention, was emptying him of life, was "pumping away" something of his individuality.'[1] Unfortunately, the excess of effort seems to have defeated his ends; today the portrait is so dark as to be almost invisible.

The sufferings Whistler underwent when painting a portrait increased rather than lessened towards the end of his life, and the *Portrait of A. J. Eddy* (Chicago Art Institute), on which he commenced work in 1894, was not finished for several years. Another long drawn-out affair was the *Arrangement in Grey and Green: Portrait of J. J. Cowan*, in the National Gallery, Edinburgh. This picture was started in Paris in May, 1893, when Cowan gave Whistler eighteen sittings and a further twelve in the September of the same year. The portrait was left for two years and in May and June of 1895 he stood for it twelve times; other sittings followed, the last apparently in 1901, but after some sixty sittings, it remained unfinished. Although instructions were left that it was not to be given to the sitter, it was excluded from the list of works to be destroyed after his death. Much time was also spent on the lovely *Rose et Vert, L'Iris: Miss Kinsella* (Mrs Bruce Durham, Basingstoke, Hampshire), which was started in 1893 and shown in the Salon at the Champs de Mars in 1904. The picture shows signs of labour; nevertheless, the suggestion of movement and growth which it contains has a feeling not dissimilar from that found in certain works by Rodin and accords with the *fin de siècle* spirit of an artist like Klimt. His relentless search for perfection is illustrated in this picture. Moreover, in spite of Mrs Whistler's influence, he was involved in troubles: the quarrel with Sir William Eden over the portrait *Brown and Gold: Lady Eden*, which also embroiled him with George Moore (whom he challenged to a duel!), is a familiar tale. The partially destroyed portrait is in the Birnie Philip Bequest, Glasgow.

As far as his full-length portraits were concerned, Whistler seems to have reached a stage beyond which he found it hard to go. He had continually to refine, as it were, upon a formula which was already established. Thus he almost invariably

[1] July, 1891. *Pages from the Goncourt Journal*, ed. Robert Baldick, 1962, p. 366.

56 GEORGE W. VANDERBILT.

Canvas, 80 × 37 *in. About* 1897.
National Gallery of Art, Washington.

57 ROSE AND VIOLET:
CARMEN QUI RIT.
Canvas, 22⅝ × 17⅜ *in. Late* 1890s.
*Birnie Philip Bequest, University of
Glasgow.*

58 GOLD AND BROWN: SELF PORTRAIT.
Canvas, $25\frac{1}{2} \times 18\frac{1}{2}$ *in. Butterfly signature. About* 1900. *National Gallery of Art, Washington.*

remained faithful to his customary way of painting a full-length female portrait, as may be seen from the *Harmony in Black: Mrs Charles Whibley*, at the City Art Gallery, Glasgow. Yet this picture and the *Rose et Or: La Tulipe: Miss Ethel Birnie Philip*, in the Birnie Philip Bequest, Glasgow, in spite of their undoubted charm and elegance, lack a sort of inner conviction: they are a shade mechanical. At this stage, he seems to have been much happier with small intimate interiors like the *Ethel Philip reading* (Fig. 53), also in the Birnie Philip Bequest, Glasgow, which dates from 1894.

In the 1890s Whistler was not in a position to go forward; and as he was over fifty, a certain lessening of his energy was only to be expected. For instance, in 1892 an attempt was made to persuade him to undertake a large panel on the stairs of the Boston Public Library, but, as the Pennells observed: 'He made notes and suggestions for the design, which, he told us, was to be a great peacock ten feet high, but the work was put off and, in the end, nothing came of the first great opportunity given him for mural decoration since the Peacock Room.'[1] Significantly in commenting on the 1892 Paris exhibition, Camille Pissarro reported to his son: 'I supposed this exhibition of Whistler would show his new works. It's strange that Whistler doesn't want to show his new canvases. Perhaps he hasn't any! For years now I have seen the same works again and again, even very early works! . . . Why?'[2] It was not that his self-confidence was damaged by the various knocks he had received; nevertheless he seems to have experienced a sense of incapacity about realising his ambitions; consequently he beat a retreat towards a greater and more captivating cult of refinement. This is noticeable in his small intimate portraits.

His pandering to his own legend was also a little overdone; perhaps, if anything, he had grown too inward. The following description of him in his Paris days, given by A. J. Eddy, a very shrewd observer, is certainly revealing: 'If in his studio, Whistler would first turn to the wall every picture and arrange the few pieces of furniture so that nothing should attract the vagrant eye, then he would place the one picture he wished seen on the easel in the best of light, without, however, letting it be seen until frame and glass were carefully wiped, when, stepping back on a line with his visitor, he, too, would enjoy his work as if he saw it for the first time. He would never exhibit anything he was tired of, and he never tired of anything he exhibited. This appreciation of his own work, his enthusiasm over what he had done, was often misunderstood by people accustomed to the false modesty of artists who stand dumb while others vainly strive to see in their work the beauties which they of all people can best make known. If time permitted he might bring forth two, or even three, pictures, but rarely more, and always each by itself.'[3]

[1] Pennell, II, p. 132.   [2] Op. cit., p. 195. (Letter of 17th April.)
[3] Op. cit., pp. 134–5.

It was all very well for Whistler to refuse to talk to a visitor until he had changed his tie or, as occurred one day at luncheon, angrily getting rid of a Japanese plate because its colour did not match the grilled salmon on it.[1] Yet his attempt to create an atmosphere, which kept him out of contact with anything likely to upset him, tempting though it might be, held risks. It carried with it the danger that he could lose an essential vitality; he could become almost the inmate, the recluse of a sheltered bower. This withdrawal did occur; and one feels his sympathy with the attitude expressed in Mallarmé's well-known lines: *Hélas, hélas, j'ai lu tous les livres*; not, of course, that he was a great reader. Perhaps it is a question of balance and proportion; there is a middle position between a passionate cult of an ideal in art and a complete devotion to realism, and Whistler tended to tip the scale in one direction to the exclusion of the other.

A significant statement made in these years draws attention to the sort of shadowy, dreamy world he inhabited. 'As the light fades and the shadows deepen all petty and exacting details vanish, everything trivial disappears, and I see things as they are in great strong masses: the buttons are lost, but the sitter remains, the garment is lost, but the sitter remains; the sitter is lost, but the shadow remains; the shadow is lost, but the picture remains. And that, night cannot efface from the painter's imagination.'[2] He was relying on his memory in such pictures; the ascent into Axel's tower and the bolting of the door is also implicit; and there is something pessimistic about his devotion to this obscure world.

The artist himself was evidently conscious of the difficulties of his position and two of the series of letters which he wrote to Beatrix from Lyme Regis, Dorset, in the late summer of 1895, suggest that he was then undergoing some sort of artistic crisis; its exact nature is by no means easy to define owing to the exalted tone of his language; but he evidently felt that his inspiration (his 'Goddess', as he called it) was on the wane. This correspondence, the publication of which is not possible owing to the terms of the Birnie Philip Bequest, reveals that Whistler had been a prey to doubt and uncertainty and that, during his time alone, he had found his old self criticism appearing once again. Nevertheless, it does appear as if he considered that these misgivings had been overcome. Yet how one wishes that he had been rather more explicit as to what had happened and in what way he saw this new departure. The few pictures he painted while in Dorset—the *Master Smith*, the *Little Rose* (both in the Museum of Fine Arts, Boston) and the *Little Forge, Lyme Regis* (Glasgow)—are not all that dissimilar from his other works; however, it is not entirely fanciful to see in their broader handling, the sign of a closer contact between the artist and his sitter. Possibly, too, the fact that he adopted a smaller scale may have enabled him to reduce his painstaking search for the tonalities within a large area: such pictures are a little

[1] This was witnessed by Octave Maus. See C. Morice, op. cit., p. 15, note.
[2] Eddy, op. cit., p. 214.

more spontaneous in effect. His sense of paint was also a shade livelier and richer, as in the *Sketch for a Self Portrait*, in the Birnie Philip Bequest, Glasgow, with its use of crisp broad highlights on the face and collar; this is one of the two first trials for the *Gold and Brown: Self Portrait* (Fig. 58), formerly in the Vanderbilt collection and now in the National Gallery, Washington.

His life was sadly and horribly changed when in May, 1896, Mrs Whistler died—a victim of incurable cancer. He had hidden from the world the anguish he had gone through in the months prior to her death: and there is a heartrending description of the painter on her last day, running across Hampstead Heath adjacent to where he and the dying woman were then living. A friend met him thus; he looked at nothing, saw no one. When he stopped him, Whistler said: 'Don't speak, don't speak. It is terrible.'[1] That she meant much to him, that she gave him peace and a measure of inspiration, that he loved her, deeply loved her, is sometimes forgotten: the extent of his loss was clearly overpowering. Sickert summed up their relationship in a tender and warm letter of condolence, sent from Venice: 'My dearest Jimmy. You must always remember now how you made her life, from the moment you took it up, absolutely perfect and happy. Your love has been as perfect and whole as your work and that is the utmost that can be achieved. Nor has her exquisite comprehension of you, and companionship with you ceased now. Never let yourself forget that her spirit is at your side now, and will always be, for sanity, and gaiety, and work; and you must not fail her now either in your hardest peril.'[2]

Sickert's letter is remarkable not only on account of its human understanding but for its understanding of that particular human being: Whistler. He clearly realised the extent to which Whistler relied on his wife and the way in which he had to keep going by work. The depth of his love for Trixie was also revealed in a moving letter Whistler himself wrote to Freer on March 24th, 1897.

The last six years of Whistler's life, though restless and disturbed, with ill health gradually gaining the upper hand, were by no means inactive; indeed, the final phase of his career was marked by a number of enterprises, ranging from the formation in 1898 of an agency called the Company of the Butterfly with an office at 2, Hinde Street, Manchester Square, London, which was designed to sell his work but which met with small success, to the foundation of an art school in Paris. This was opened at 6, Passage Stanislas, under the supervision of his model, Carmen Rossi, whose portrait he painted, and was generally known, after her name, as the Académie Carmen. The starting of such a school obviously provided Whistler with an opportunity to impose his will and to preach his ideas, both of which he liked doing, but he was by no means an ideal teacher. What he taught was summed up in his words that 'One's study, even the most unpre-

---

[1] Pennell, II, p. 172.
[2] Letter from 940 Calle del Frati Zatteri (1896). Glasgow University.

tentious, is always one's picture, and must be, in form and arrangement, a perfect harmony from the beginning'.[1] In the instructions sent to the *massière*, Miss Bate, he stated in a most dictatorial fashion that 'Mr Whistler expects, as the only acknowledgement that can be made him, complete acquiescence in his wishes—and perfect loyalty—any doubtful hesitation being quite out of place and impossible among the distinguished pupils it is his pleasure to meet'.[2] Although the school survived for a time and produced a crop of students working in the Whistlerian style, it petered out and he closed it down in 1901.

In 1898, also, he became Chairman of the executive council of the International Society of Sculptors, Painters and Gravers and subsequently its President. Thus he was partly responsible for the two important exhibitions held at the Prince's Skating Club in that year and in 1899, and which included not only his own work but examples of Bonnard, Manet, Rodin, Monet, Sisley and Toulouse-Lautrec. He took a good deal of trouble about the exhibitions and he reported to Pennell in 1898 that 'poor old Thaulow, I met him in great anxiety about his works and promised him that he should have them in a group together'.[3] These two exhibitions, which were a revelation to many young artists, did much to facilitate the accceptance of modern foreign art in England.

Such outside activities did not prevent him continuing with his artistic endeavours. There is a rather moving account of Whistler in the late 1890s by the sharp-nosed young William Rothenstein, who after dining with him returned to his studio in the rue Notre Dame des Champs: 'Climbing the stairs we found the studio in darkness. Whistler lighted a single candle. He had been gay enough during dinner, but now he became very quiet and intent, as though he forgot me. Turning a canvas that faced the wall, he examined it carefully, up and down, with the candle held near it, and then did the like with some others, peering closely into each. There was something tragic, almost frightening, as I stood and waited, in watching Whistler; he looked suddenly old, as he held the candle with trembling hands, and stared at his work, while our shapes threw restless, fantastic shadows, all around us. As I followed him silently down the stairs I realised that even Whistler must often have felt his heart heavy with the sense of failure.'[4] Yet Whistler himself did not openly acknowledge this situation; he wrote to the Pennells from Paris that 'I could almost laugh at the extraordinary progress I am making and the lovely things I am inventing—work beyond anything I have ever done before'.[5]

The question of whether or not Whistler's final works appeal is naturally a matter of taste; certainly he had by no means given up. An interesting group of pictures which date from 1899 are the nudes which in some ways hark back to

[1] Pennell, II, p. 232.   [2] Written to Miss Bate on 9th September, 1899. Glasgow University.
[3] 3rd (?) April, 1898. Freer Gallery, Washington.
[4] *Men and Memories*, 2 vols., 1931–32. Vol. I, pp. 109–10.   [5] Pennell, II, p. 203.

the 'Six Projects' of the 1860s; but the differences are quite considerable. He had abandoned the sketchy and elegant swirl of line and colour used in these pictures for a more mysterious effect; one of the most interesting was the *Purple and Gold: Phryne the Superb: Builder of Temples* (Fig. 54), in the Freer Gallery, Washington, which was exhibited at the International Society in 1901 and at the Salon of 1902. He was proud of this picture of the celebrated Athenian courtesan, which was admired by the poet Vielé-Griffin,[1] and, as the Pennells reported, he declared: 'Would she be more superb—more truly the Builder of Temples—had I painted her what is called life-size by the foolish critics who always bring out their foot-rule? Is it a question of feet and inches when you look at her?'[2] The picture itself, shrouded and mysterious, is enigmatic and contains curious erotic undertones; once again it underlines his connection with the symbolist movement and reminds us that at the time a love of the curious was widespread. Thus a critic like Octave Mirbeau, who at first had not appreciated Redon's work, was prepared by the 1890s to talk about the existence of *le mystère* in art.[3] Whistler, in fact, had turned to the nude with fresh delight; this may be seen in the many drawings and pastels which he made of the model who served for this picture, and which were mainly done from memory. His return to his old themes emphasised that he was still haunted by the 'ideal' beauty which tantalised him earlier on.

In his final years he showed a decided interest in adolescence—or, perhaps one should say, with the mystery of adolescence. By a strange paradox, although he seems to have neglected the child Jo bore him, he is always said to have been specially fond of children; however, Mrs Swanwick remembered that when young she disliked him.[4] Towards the end of his life, he quite clearly developed a real passion for painting young girls, and, in this connection, it is perhaps relevant that he greatly admired Degas's bronze of the dancer in her *tutu*. Various reasons might be advanced to explain this predilection on his part; and it is perhaps just worth drawing attention to the fact that in *La Peur de l'Amour*, a typical novel of the time, Henri de Regnier in his portrait of Whistler as 'Cyrille Buttelet' has a passage about him which is possibly susceptible of more than one interpretation. Yet it would be dangerous to read too much into a casual remark.

Whistler's range in such sketches was wide. Some like the *Blue and Coral: Little Blue Bonnet* (collection of Mrs H. L. Maxwell, New York) recall the eighteenth century; others as might be expected reflect the influence of Velasquez, and are also close to Carrière. He rendered a variety of moods—the incipient devilry of a *jeune fille en fleur*, as in the *Harmony in Blue and Violet: Miss Millie*

[1] See a letter by Whistler (in Freer's hand) from The Hague, 28th July, 1902, Freer Gallery, Washington.

[2] Pennell, II, p. 206.

[3] Letter to O. Redon, 1896. See *Lettres à Odilon Redon*, ed. R. Bacon, 1960, p. 249.

[4] Op. cit., 1935, p. 129.

Finch (Birnie Philip Bequest, Glasgow), the strange inner world of childhood dreams as in several of the sketches, or the equivocal tantalising note of a girl already aware of life, as in *Grey and Silver: La Petite Souris* (Fig. 55: Birnie Philip Bequest, Glasgow). Such studies are principally confined to the final years of his life. But he still continued to paint his small open-air sketches; his passion for the sea did not lessen.

The series of seascapes painted at Pourville in the summer of 1899 are especially brilliant, and in the *Gold and Green: Pourville* (Freer Gallery, Washington) he returned to a motif—a single figure on the beach—which he had painted over thirty years before. In such pictures the colour became increasingly evocative, though the composition was on a small scale, as may be seen in the *Grey and Gold: The Golden Bay, Ireland* (formerly Messrs Agnew), which was painted in 1900; in fact, the almost abstract areas of colour in this work or the *Ajaccio* in the Fogg Museum, Cambridge, painted in 1901, are by no means dissimilar from the approach used by Kandinsky a few years later, due allowance being made for the differences in tonality. Large-scale enterprises, when undertaken, were almost beyond him; however, he had not lost his knack of finding an effective pose, and his *George W. Vanderbilt* (Fig. 56: National Gallery, Washington), in spite of its poor condition, is remarkable; the careful positioning of the figure with his right leg jutting out so as to set up a contrast with the dado, indicates that he was keener than before on perspective. This picture, which is little known, is quite fascinating with its sense of uneasy space. It is not easy to read and it is with some difficulty that one realises that the sitter is holding a hat in his right hand. It is most refined and Vanderbilt becomes a sort of Proustian figure—an American Swann.

The various heads of Carmen Rossi (Fig. 57), the troublesome model at his Paris school, are robust and recall the realistic style of the 1850s, but the portrait of the *Rose and Brown: The Philosopher C. E. Holloway*, in the collection of the Comte de Ganay, Paris, is more delicate and atmospheric. Moreover, the portraits of his sister-in-law, Miss Birnie Philip, now at Glasgow, combine a sharp grasp of a very decided character with his usual harmonious tonal painting. And one of the most striking pictures was his *Gold and Brown: Self Portrait*, in the Birnie Philip Bequest, Glasgow; certainly under way in May, 1898, this seems to have been based on Velasquez's *Pablo de Valladolid* in the Prado, a photograph of which belonged to him: it is a searching document. His sense of character did not desert him at the end; and it transpires in the small but excellent head of the gambler Canfield of 1902 (present whereabouts unknown), which brings out his craftiness, and in the intense but vibrant unfinished head of C. L. Freer in the Freer Gallery, Washington, who was the enthusiastic collector of his work. In these years, Arthur Symons caught Whistler's spirit in a vivid passage: 'I never saw anyone so feverishly alive as this little, old man, with his bright, withered cheeks, over which the skin was drawn tightly, his darting eyes, under their prickly bushes of eyebrows, his fantastically creased black and white curls of hair, his bitter and subtle mouth, and, above all, his exquisite hands, never at rest'[1] His powers did not wane even at the end; so much is clear from the *Dorothy Seton, A Daughter of Eve* (Birnie Philip Bequest, Glasgow), a particularly full-blooded and handsome small picture, and one of his final works. He died in London in 1903.

[1] *Studies in Seven Arts*, 1906, p. 71.

❧ ELEVEN ❧

Finale

WHISTLER was more American than he realised himself or than he acknowledged. Indeed A. J. Eddy, that perceptive critic, in his brilliant book on him underlined the connection by pointing out that: 'The Puritan element which is to be found in every American achievement, whether in war, in art, or in literature, though often deeply hidden, is conspicuous in Whistler's work, though he himself would probably have been the first to deny it; and it is this element of sobriety, of steadfastness, of undeviating adherence to convictions and ideals, that constitutes the firm foundation of his art, of his many brilliant and beautiful superstructures of fancy.'[1] One has only to look at the portrait of his mother to realise that this is essentially an American picture, painted, however, in a European language. And this impression arises as much from its muted tones as from the features of Mrs Whistler—a typical New England lady of the last century.

Any attempt to draw too close a parallel between Whistler and his American contemporaries or to single out the American component in his outlook and style is a perilous undertaking. Nevertheless, this does exist. Even a casual acquaintance with the New England landscape or with the coastline near Baltimore (which may be glimpsed as the train travels from that city to New York) does suggest that the character of the light in his pictures owes something, at any rate, to his native land. The austerity of his portraits carries some relationship to those by Thomas Eakins and, like Winslow Homer, he loved the sea, though he did not paint the rough ice-cold waves that pound on the East Coast, which were so loved by this artist. American, too, was his interest in, and affection for, the Far East, though his cult of Nirvana was never as explicit as that of Bigelow or John La Farge. Perhaps we may also attribute his belief in himself, that proud independence of mind, to a certain transatlantic toughness (and loneliness, too). The sense for the mystery of life may not be exclusively American, but it is to be found in Henry James and earlier in Poe; and Whistler, one ought to remember, belonged to a generation raised in the shadow of the Civil War. It was this response to the unusual, this sense that the artist may pierce through to some inner truth by suggestion and by creating an atmosphere, which related him to the hermetic world of the Symbolists, who incidentally numbered another American, Stuart Merrill, among their adherents. This was why, perhaps, Whistler shunned Impressionism, essentially an out-of-doors and robust art.

[1] Op. cit., p. 49.

His loneliness was probably inevitable. The rôle of the expatriate artist is ever complicated, as D. H. Lawrence once suggested in a brilliant story; he is cut off from his 'grass roots' and consequently he has to try to form some links with the traditions of the country in which he settles. This was Whistler's problem. He chose England rather than France, but he did not find anything in England which really held him. As he was so sure of his ideas and so insistent that he was right, he constantly tilted against the stupidity of his contemporaries (in his eyes, at any rate); he told the Pennells 'I know that many people think my nomenclature funny and myself "eccentric". Yes, "eccentric" is the adjective they find for me'.[1] He might have been disappointed if they had not done so; his opinions and costumes were certainly ammunition for the conventional.

With Whistler, the Puritan was complemented by the Dandy and the Prophet. The rôle of the perfectionist is always an ungrateful one and the aims he set himself were laudable if devilishly hard to achieve: a portrait style measuring up to the great masters, Velasquez or Hals, for instance, and a sense of tonal values akin to that of the Dutch cabinet painters. He tried to capture something else beside— the fleeting quality of individuality which in every human being reflects the throb of the inner life. But was he able to persist with his endeavours? Eddy once again put his finger on part of his trouble, of the trouble which must arise when a painter works to command as well as for pleasure. 'He could never work at an etching, a lithograph or a painting, one moment after it had become drudgery', were his words; 'he could never finish a thing simply because he had begun it, or because someone thought it ought to be finished; hence endless misunderstandings, with sitters and patrons, who could not understand why what they had bargained for should not be finished and delivered.'[2]

His perfectionism was accompanied by a delight in, and a need for, elegance. This perhaps is an aspect of his work which has caused him to be misunderstood and even despised in our period. The cult of elegance was implicit in all he undertook; it can be clearly seen in his own setting. All through his life, he can be found trying to make an attractive nest: those plain distempered walls, those Chinese pots, those Japanese prints, the eighteenth-century silver, the Chippendale, Sheraton and Empire furniture—all were present so as to provide an appropriate background for the Butterfly. This attitude to his setting as to his life sprang from the demands of a cultivated and fastidious personality who delighted in rare experiences and, as a matter of right, sought out the delicate and the refined.

An artist's cultivation of elegance is a question of temperament. Just as some natures delight in the correct cut of a dress or a proper shade of colour, others respond to an exquisite profile (as did the artists of Amarna) or the depiction in colours of the sheen of silks and satins. There is no reason against the artist doing so. Nevertheless, he had to walk a tightrope between an absorption in elegance

[1] Pennell, I, p. 180.   [2] Op. cit., pp. 90–1.

for its modish character and one which possesses an artistic quality. A contrast, for instance, between Boldini, Helleu and Whistler points to the difference in achievement, if not in intention, between these three men. What is reasonably clear is that Whistler was after a more profound means of expression. Yet he was not a robust painter and his turning away from Courbet's realism was understandable in terms of his own personality. So, given his attitude, was his failure to find any real point of contact with 'ideal' painting and with the classicistic revival: unlike Puvis de Chavannes, Hans von Marées or Leighton, he could not derive sustained nourishment from a classical past; and significantly when he did turn to antiquity, he turned to Tanagra figurines and the Hellenistic style. He did not demonstrably appreciate the great phases of Greek sculpture, which Pater wrote about so well at the time.

Whistler maintained that an artist transcended his period. However, in some respect, his work partly reflects the cosmopolitan decadent trend of the 1880s and 1890s. Arthur Symons once observed of the *fin de siècle* in his age that: 'After a fashion it is no doubt a decadence; it has all the qualities that mark the end of great periods, the qualities that we find in the Greek, the Latin, decadence: an intense self-consciousness, a restless curiosity in research, an over subtilizing refinement upon refinement, a spiritual and moral perversity.'[1] The last element is not really discernible in Whistler's art, even though an acute Austrian critic like Hevesi[2] did discover this sort of twist in it. However, the 'subtilizing refinement upon refinement' is typical of his work. He was both a man of the 90s and an opponent of some of its main manifestations. Thus while loving yellow and recognising the merit in Beardsley's drawings, he did not care for *The Yellow Book*. And he can hardly be claimed as an exponent of *Art Nouveau*; even if certain aspects of his contribution offer points of contact with this movement—the Peacock Room, the affection for *Japonaiserie*, and his typography. But his sketch for Loïe Fuller in the Birnie Philip Bequest at Glasgow underlines the differences between his style and *Art Nouveau*.

His art has been out of favour for so long that it is proper to ask if it has anything to recommend it to our generation, or if, on the contrary, it suffers from the weariness of the *fin de siècle*. A certain wanness is sometimes present in his work, but his essential qualities remain nonetheless. The scope of his achievement is greater than is currently admitted. He was a force in creating a new look for interior decoration and typography—this is not the least of his achievements, and one, incidentally, which still bears fruit. As a portrait painter, his contribution, though not of the highest order, was effective, and half-a-dozen pictures are finer than anything painted in England at the time. They show, too, that a portrait

[1] *Harper's Magazine*, lxxxviii (November, 1893), p. 858.
[2] See *Altkunst-Neukunst*, 1909, pp. 477–482. Hevesi also makes the point that Klimt had learnt much from him.

V.   ARRANGEMENT IN GREY AND BLACK, No. 2: THOMAS CARLYLE. Canvas ($67\frac{3}{8}$ x $56\frac{1}{2}$ in.).
Signed on the right with a butterfly in a circle. This is one of the artist's most famous pictures
and reveals the influence of Velasquez. It was bought by the Corporation of Glasgow from
the artist in March, 1891, for 1000 guineas, as the result of a petition by a group of artists of the
Glasgow School (Glasgow Art Gallery and Museum).

painter in the late nineteenth century could practise a traditional manner without falling into the traps of plagiarism or pastiche. He was an artist also who managed to capture personality, to evoke the inner life of a sitter and yet not to forget the visual appeal of the subject.

Whistler was a wise colourist. He obviously realised that the succulent colours of a Rubens or the warm refulgent hues of the Venetians were not for him, and the Impressionist use of colour did not tempt him; it did not correspond to his vision. He grasped, shrewd and determined as he was, that his ambitions could be best secured by employing a lower *gamme* of colour—but one no less challenging because of its restrictions. And he was sensible not to have ventured into realms beyond his capacities. His feeling for colour, within this range, was exceedingly refined and true. '*Et parfois,*' Proust once wrote, '*sur le ciel et la mer uniformément gris, un peu de rose s'ajoutait avec un raffinement exquis, cependant qu'un petit papillon qui s'était endormi au bas de la fenêtre semblait apposer avec ses ailes au bas de cette "harmonie gris et rose", dans le goût de celles de Whistler, la signature favorite du maître de Chelsea.*'[1] Whistler realised as well that grey is a colour which can last a painter a lifetime; fortunately he was prepared to chase the shades that lured him—and in the panels the results were opalescent, delicate notes, justly and delicately secured.

For modern taste, Whistler's use of a low range of tonalities has seemed a little depressing, but his own words on the reason for this are interesting. Thus he said:[2] 'The notion that I paint flesh lower in tone than it is in nature is entirely based upon the popular superstition as to what flesh really is—when seen on canvas; for the people never look at nature with any sense of its pictorial appearance, for which reason, by the way, they also never look at a picture with any sense of nature, but, unconsciously from habit, with reference to what they have seen in other pictures....' It was, he argued, the artist's aim to make people 'stand out' from the frame. And, he went on: 'Whereas, could the people be induced to turn their eyes but for a moment with the fresh power of comparison upon their fellow creatures as they pass in the gallery, they might be made dimly to perceive (though I doubt it, so blind is their belief in the bad) how little they resemble the impudent images on the walls! how "quiet" in colours they are! how grey!!! how "low in tone".'

'My friends,' he is reported as saying, 'have you noticed the way in which a musician cares for his violin—how beautiful it is. How well kept? How tenderly handled? Your palette is your instrument, its colours the notes, and upon it you play your symphonies.'[3] Hence the care he gave to the arrangement of his tones prior to the attack: the artist, for him, had to have the vision in his eyes at the start and then work towards the ideal; the artist had to contrive. Thus, too, his ideal of

---

[1] *A l'ombre des jeunes filles en fleurs*, Vol. III, pp. 58–9.

[2] Cited by W. Dowdeswell, 'Whistler' in *The Art Journal*, xxxix (1897), p. 100.

[3] E. S. Crawford 'The Gentler Side of Mr Whistler' in *The Reader*, ii (September, 1903), pp. 387–90. Quoted by Eddy, p. 278. Crawford had been a pupil of Whistler's.

space was contingent upon giving deliberate assistance to Nature; the spatial conception of the Nocturnes, partly derived from the Japanese, was one that resulted in tasteful arrangements; nevertheless, artificiality, as such, was avoided owing to the origin of the inspiration in observation. So it was with his portraits. In his Paris studio the skylight was so well managed with its shades that he could keep the light soft and constant so that the sitter loomed up in the shadow and was then placed, receding behind the frame; many, in fact, are the accounts of his attempts to discover the proper, rewarding method of arranging his portraits.

'As music is the poetry of sound, so painting is the poetry of sight, and the subject matter has nothing to do with the harmony of sound or of colour.' These famous words sum up his artistic conceptions and accordingly he delighted in arrangement of colours and shapes; this delight, to a certain extent, gives his painting its abstract quality—a term which was employed in connection with it during his lifetime. His Nocturnes reveal his delicate sense of colour and his feeling for space—for an almost abstract space. Once again his flair, in this case his perception of the links between the East and West, revealed his nose for a salient trend in his age, as well as his own gift for assimilation. In their own right, these are subtle and delicate pictures, finely suggestive of a mood; but it is one that arises not so much from the subject matter as from a solicitude for the properties of painting. The Nocturnes also show how Whistler shared in the reaction against traditional Renaissance perspective, a trend which included artists like Puvis de Chavannes and Gauguin.

As a technician he did not always succeed—the state of a number of his pictures is a proof of his failures. Yet he did seek to enlarge the artist's processes; for instance, Rennell Rodd remembered that he experimented 'a good deal with petroleum as a medium, painting with brushes more than two feet long which he held by the extreme end in his nervous, delicate fingers, surveying his pictures and his model across the length of the studio, and then dashing up at a run to place the telling stroke on the canvas.'[1] Too much may be made of the relationship between certain of his works and the procedures of action painting; and in the long run the results were very different.

In some respects he was close to Impressionism, but he never espoused its principles. Some of his pictures were described as impressionist, a term which he implicitly rejected in a note to the *Crepuscule in Opal: Trouville* (Toledo Museum of Art), which was shown at the Goupil Gallery in 1892 as No. 39. The reason for this designation was not far to seek. It can be found in the critical concepts of the time. In the late 1880s and 1890s, many considered that the emergence of a new trend of realism or naturalism, looking back to the example of a painter like Velasquez, constituted an impressionist style.

Confirmation of this attitude may be found in R. A. M. Stevenson's volume

[1] *Social and Diplomatic Memories*, 1922, 2 vols. Vol. I, p. 17.

on Velasquez—that epoch-making book in art critical circles—which was first published in 1895 and a copy of which, incidentally, belonged to Whistler. In his subtle assessment of the Spanish Master, Stevenson consistently called him an impressionist, a term which, by extension, he used to include Whistler and Carolus-Duran, as well as several of those French painters more usually considered as being proper Impressionists and who exhibited with the Impressionist group. The tenor of his volume was that technique *is* art, a concept which must surely have won Whistler's approval, and, as Stevenson said: 'Technique in painting, then, must be understood as the method of using any medium of expression so as to bring out the character of a decorative pattern, or to convey the sentiment with which you regard some appearances of the external world.'[1] For Stevenson, the appropriate technique for the modern artist was impressionism. The essence of impressionism, as he understood it, had nothing to do with the dissolution of light and the use of raw colours, as practised by the French: it lay in the observation of every part of the picture in subservience to the whole. This is what he found in Velasquez. His view was shared by Whistler and, insofar as Stevenson's definition of impressionism is accepted as one possible way of explaining the term, then Whistler was an impressionist. Inevitably, the fact that Nature was the basis for his art and that he aimed at a selective view of what lay before him meant at times, and in certain specific works, that affinities existed between his approach and that of the Impressionists proper. This occurred mainly when he worked direct from Nature, as with the etchings executed in Venice and the following years.

In this connection, it is worth quoting the statement which Whistler gave to the *Pall Mall Gazette*,[2] although the Pennells were by no means certain that he was reported correctly. In this he said to the journalist who visited him in 1890 after his return from Holland: 'First you see me at work on the Thames (producing one of the famous series). Now, there you see the crude and hard detail of the beginner. So far, so good. There, you see, all is sacrificed to exactitude of outline. Presently, and almost unconsciously, I begin to criticise myself, and to feel the craving of the artist for form and colour. The result was the second stage, which my enemies call inchoate, and I call Impressionism. The third stage I have shown you. In that I have endeavoured to combine stages one and two. You have the elaboration of the first stage, and the quality of the second.'

Whistler's flair for modernity was considerable. Thus he by no means shut his eyes to what was going on and to some extent his art was related both to Impressionism and Symbolism, with which he had more temperamental affinities. But he was never altogether absorbed by them; his individuality and firm streak of independence always meant that he had to follow his own route; no other way was open to him. His originality certainly resulted in the creation of a personal style—one that was endorsed by numerous followers in England. One can hardly

---

[1] Op. cit., p. 81.   [2] 4th March, 1890. Quoted Pennell, II, p. 84.

think of the early Sickert, Steer or Gilman without remembering him, and his influence was considerable in Scotland. Abroad his impact was also strong— Hammershøj, Picasso,[1] Van Rysselberghe are some of the artists indebted to him.

In 1912 Ezra Pound declared that he claimed Whistler as 'our own great artist, and even this informal salute, drastic as it is, may not be out of place at the threshold of what I hope is an endeavour to carry into our American poetry the same sort of life and intensity which he infused into modern painting'.[2] Pound, I think, underlines one of the qualities which makes us turn again to Whistler— his way of heightening our apprehension of life, paradoxically, not by any bold extrovert manner of painting, but by forcing us to recognise that harmony may derive from an arrangement of forms and colours. This is the beauty of the finest Nocturnes, portraits and pastels; a delight in perfection is the key note. 'You have done too much of the exquisite', wrote Henry James,[3] 'not to have earned more despair, than anything else, but don't doubt that something vibrates back when that exquisite takes the form of recognition of a not utterly indelicate brother'. His was an art which stemmed from life, from observation, from contact with reality, yet he sought to render something which could only come from the selection practised by a poetical eye; and as Stevenson said: 'He works in the interest of a lofty mistress far withdrawn from the eye of common curiosity, and it is at her bidding that he cares for no knowledge, excitements, emotions, facts or beauties that will not serve the divine and eternal beauty of style.'[4]

The moment of retreat from day, the moment when light dissolves and takes wing, when the *heure bleue* intervenes, this beautiful and terrible moment, half sad, half delightful, he made all his own: this is the moment when man, left to himself, may perceive the truth, the ironic truth, of life. It is one of Whistler's achievements to make us grasp the melancholy as well as the poetry of nightfall.

[1] Cf. A. Blunt and Phoebe Pool. *Picasso: The Formative Years*, 1962.

[2] Letter to Harriet Monroe, 18th August, 1912: see the *Letters of Ezra Pound 1907–1941*, ed. D. D. Paige, 1951, p. 44.

[3] Letter of 25th February, 1897. Glasgow University.

[4] *The Pall Mall Gazette*, 11th December, 1895.

Index

Numbers in italics indicate pages on which illustrations appear in the text; numbers in parenthesis indicate plate numbers.

DAT